TO:

....

FROM:

....

DATE:

....

HOW GREAT IS OUR GOD

100 INDESCRIBABLE DEVOTIONS ABOUT GOD AND SCIENCE

LOUIE GIGLIO

WITH TAMA FORTNER

ILLUSTRATED BY
NICOLA ANDERSON

 passionpublishing Tommy NELSON

An Imprint of Thomas Nelson

CONTENTS

INTRODUCTION

Hi, friend!

My name is Pastor Louie. We may have met before if you've read my previous kids' book, *Indescribable*, or maybe you or your parents picked up this book because, like me, you want to learn more about God and the incredible things He makes.

But do you want to know something that blows my mind? You and I can never learn everything there is to know about God. He's limitless, which means there's always something more to discover about Him! That's why scientists, astronomers, doctors, and researchers are always uncovering new things about His creation—in the depths of the universe and in the world around us. Like figuring out how something glows in the dark. Or finding the blue supergiant star we named Rigel. Or learning what makes a bloodhound such an excellent tracker.

Like *Indescribable*, the book you're holding is filled with 100 devotions, and each one focuses on a unique and incredible thing God created throughout the universe. God's Word, the Bible, says that even though we can't see God with our physical eyes, we can learn what He is like by seeing and studying everything He has made (Romans 1:20). That means all of creation—from the far-away stars that only the strongest telescope can see to the tiniest cells in your pinky toenail—tells us something about God.

I think God is delighted when we focus our minds and hearts on learning about Him and what He has made. I hope these devotions help you do just that! I've asked some trusted friends to join us on the journey. (You may remember them from *Indescribable*!) Meet six kids who are growing and learning just like you: Evyn, Raz, Norah, Joshua, Clarke, and Adelynn.

Each day we'll read together about a different part of God's creation, be amazed by scientific facts, talk with God in prayer, and grow deeper in knowledge that will fill up our hearts and our minds.

If you'd like to focus on learning about a specific part of creation, feel free to skip to different parts of the book. We'll talk about four major topics:

As you read, remember that the same God who made you and knows everything about you is inviting you to know and learn about Him. I'm so glad you're on this journey with me to discover more of who He is. God has so much in store for you.

Enjoy the adventure ahead!

Pastor Louie

1

THIS ONE IS *JUUUST* RIGHT!

> Who knows, you may have been chosen
> queen for just such a time as this.
>
> —ESTHER 4:14 ICB

You remember the story about Goldilocks and the three bears, right? While Mama, Papa, and Baby Bear are out for a walk, Goldilocks helps herself to their porridge, chairs, and beds, testing each one in turn until she finds the one that's *"juuust* right." While Goldilocks could learn a thing or two about manners, there's something to be said for things being just right. Like our Earth. It's in just the right spot for life—a place scientists call the *Goldilocks Zone,* or the *Habitable Zone* for you more scientific types. Earth isn't too close to the Sun (which would burn us to a crisp) or too far away (which would turn our planet into a big, round popsicle).

In all the vastness of space, God placed Earth in just the right spot for life. And guess what else—God places each of His people in just the right spot, just as carefully. Like long ago when He placed Queen Esther in just the right spot to save her people. You can read this incredible story in the Old Testament book of Esther.

Now, you might look up at all the stars—or even at all the 7.6 billion people in the world—and start to feel very small, maybe even unimportant. But remember this: the God of all creation chose you to be His own, and He put you in the right spot to play an important part in His kingdom. Yes, you may be small, but you are prized by Majesty. And you have been sent for by the God of all creation. Now, how great is that?

Dear God, when I start to feel small or unimportant, help me remember that You made me just right and chose me to be Yours.

HOW GREAT!

Fifteen different "Goldilocks" factors make conditions perfect for life on Earth—things like how much water we have, the Moon's pull on the Earth, our spot in the Milky Way galaxy, and more. The fact that Earth meets these conditions is so amazing that some astronomers have estimated the chances of there being another planet like ours in the universe to be around 1 in 700 quintillion—or 1 in 700,000,000,000,000,000,000!

2

THAT'S IMPOSSIBLE!

He is the Maker of heaven and earth,
the sea, and everything in them.

— PSALM 146:6 NIV

The first verse of the Bible, Genesis 1:1, tells us that in the beginning, before there was an Earth or people or the starry sky, God existed. That same verse and the ones that follow tell us He Himself

created the heavens and the Earth . . . and *life*! Everything we see is a product of His creativity. One of the coolest things about studying science is discovering how miraculously detailed God's creation is—from the tiny hairs on your head to the massive mountains and stars.

God created living things with some essential building blocks called *peptides*. (It sounds just like it looks: PEP-tides.) When joined with other chemicals, peptides help make a cell, and cells are the basic parts of every living thing.

Peptides are so tiny that we can't see them without the help of some mega-powerful microscopes. But just because they're small doesn't mean they're simple! Each peptide is made of two or more chemical components called *amino acids*, which need to be joined in just the right way to create the variety of peptides our bodies need to function properly. The chances of that happening by accident are slim—about 1 in 10 duodecillion, or 10,000,000,000,000,000,000,000,000,000,000,000,000,000. That's a 1 with 40 zeroes after it! Sound impossible? Not with God!

God made amino acids, peptides, cells, and all of creation to show us how great and powerful He is. What's really amazing is that the same great God who designed peptides put them together in just the right way to create you!

Lord, everywhere I look I see signs of how great You are. Thank You for Your amazing creation, including me!

Peptides are in every one of the estimated 37.2 *trillion* cells in your body! There are many different types of peptides, and each has a special role in maintaining your overall health. Some peptides help your muscles grow and repair, while others carry messages throughout the body.

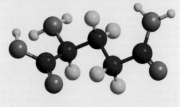

L - glutamine

PURR-FECTLY HAPPY

Be content with what you have,
because God has said, "Never will I
leave you; never will I forsake you."

—HEBREWS 13:5 NIV

A cat's purr is one of the most soothing sounds around. But it's also a little mysterious because we don't completely understand how or why they purr. We usually think cats purr because they're happy and content. And that's true. But cats purr for other reasons too. A mother cat will purr right after her kittens are born. The vibrations help the kittens, whose eyes are still closed, find the warmth and milk of their mom. Cats also purr when they're nervous or hurting. Scientists think the purrs soothe them and may even help them recover from injuries quicker.

Every cat has its own *purr*-sonality. Some are soft and rumbling, while others sound like an engine starting up from across the room. Whatever the reason behind it, purring has become a symbol for feeling happy and content.

The apostle Paul said he had learned the secret of feeling happy and content no matter what. How? By counting on Jesus (Philippians 4:12–13). He trusted Jesus to give him all he truly needed—and you can too! That doesn't mean you'll feel like turning cartwheels all the time. But it does mean you will have a blessing each day. You just might have to look up to remember it. Even on the worst days, you have a God who will never leave you and promises to meet all your needs. And those are some pretty great reasons to purr!

Lord, open my eyes to see all the reasons I have to be happy and content—and let me "purr" out my praise and thanks to You!

HOW GREAT!

House cats aren't the only cats that purr. Big cats like bobcats, cheetahs, lynxes, and even mountain lions purr too. But cats that roar (like lions, tigers, leopards, and jaguars) don't purr. That's because the bone in their throat is too hard to vibrate—unlike the more elastic bone of purring cats.

Mountain lion

STORMY WEATHER

God made rules for the rain. And he set
a path for a thunderstorm to follow.

— JOB 28:26 ICB

Howling wind. Pounding rain. Booming thunder. Lightning streaking across the sky. You know what that is—it's a storm!

Scientifically speaking, a storm is any serious disturbance in the Earth's atmosphere. There are storms of wind, hail, snow, and even dust, but the most common storms are thunderstorms. They have dark clouds, heavy rain, lightning, thunder, and strong winds. Thunderstorms happen when hot, moist air rises up and meets cooler air. As the warm air cools, clouds, rain, and lightning form. Meanwhile, the cooler air sinks toward the ground, creating strong winds. Some 1,800 thunderstorms happen across our planet every single day! And that's not counting all the other kinds of storms. Thunderstorms, snowstorms, and dust storms are all usually violent, often dangerous, and definitely scary.

But don't worry. Jesus knows a thing or two about storms. He once walked through a storm at sea—right on top of those angry waves. They didn't even slow Him down (Matthew 14:22–33). Another time, He slept through a storm, at least until His disciples woke Him up. Then He told that storm to hush and be still (Mark 4:35–41). The thing is, you're going to have storms in your life—thunderstorms, friend storms, family storms, or maybe even a faith storm. But know this: Jesus is ready to walk with you through the storms. So ask Him for help. He'll be with you from the first glimpse of storm clouds until the Sun comes out again.

Lake Maracaibo

There's a place in Venezuela, around Lake Maracaibo (mar-uh-KAHY-boh), where the storm almost never ends! For about 300 days each year, lightning zaps down an average of 28 strikes per minute and sometimes unleashes up to 3,600 bolts an hour, or one per second! Known as Catatumbo (ka-tah-TOOM-boh) lightning, this storm is so fierce and powerful that it can be seen up to 250 miles away.

Dear Lord, when storms come—in the skies, in the people around me, or in my heart—help me to remember that You are right there with me and that You are bigger than any storm!

FLOATING, FLYING, EXPLODING SEEDS!

"Plant what is right. Then you
will harvest good things."

—HOSEA 10:12 ICB

Since plants don't do much roaming around, God has given them
some unique ways to spread their seeds. You might have heard about
birds eating seeds and then, well, "leaving" them somewhere else. Some
seeds stick to an animal's fur and are spread when they eventually fall off. But
other plants are a bit more creative in sharing their seeds.

For example, the coconut is actually a gigantic seed that floats! By riding the waves, coconuts have spread their trees to islands around the world. Other seeds, like the dandelion and maple "whirlybird," sprout wings and fly away. The squirting cucumber fills with a liquid, building up pressure inside until it explodes, squirting its seeds 10 to 20 feet away. But perhaps the most impressive—and dangerous—is the sandbox tree. Also called the dynamite tree, the sandbox tree has seed pods like ticking bombs. When ready, they *explode*, shooting out their seeds at 150 miles per hour with a sound like a gunshot!

God was very creative with plants and their seeds. But there's one kind of seed He wants *you* to spread: the seed of kindness. Being kind means more than just smiling and being nice. It takes courage to be kind to that kid everybody else picks on or that person who's different from you. And it takes strength to be kind when you're tired or when others aren't so kind to you. But when you plant a seed of kindness, it grows . . . and spreads! When you're kind to someone, it encourages that person to be kind to others, who are then encouraged to be kind to still more people, and on and on. So go ahead—spread a few seeds of kindness today!

Lord, plant a seed of kindness in my heart and let it grow so big that I just have to share it with everyone I meet.

HOW GREAT!

The sandbox tree is also called the Monkey-no-climb tree because it's covered in spikey spines. The sap causes a terrible rash and even temporary blindness. It's even been used to make poison darts and arrows! You definitely don't want this tree in your backyard!

WHY IS THE SKY BLUE?

In the beginning God created the sky.

— GENESIS 1:1 ICB

Have you ever asked, "Why is the sky blue?" After all, it could have been purple or green or a lovely shade of puce. (What color is *puce* anyway?) Actually, the sky isn't blue. We only see it as blue.

The fact is, sunlight is made up of all the colors of the rainbow. The light travels in waves. Some colors of light travel in shorter waves and others in longer waves. Light also travels in a straight line until it bumps into something—like the air, bits of dust, and water vapor in our atmosphere.

Because red, orange, and yellow have longer waves, they pass on through our atmosphere without bumping into much. But blue and violet waves are shorter. They bump into everything and scatter over the sky. Because our eyes don't see violet very well, we see the blue. So, to us, the sky is blue.

With all our science and technology, we can figure out the answers to some pretty tough questions, like "Why is the sky blue?" We can learn about wavelengths and the atmosphere. But we can never figure out *everything*. Sometimes we just have to stop and say, "Wow! God did that!" The sky is blue, the grass is green, you are you, and I am me because . . . Wow! God did that!

Dear God, help me notice the blue sky so that I can stop and say, "Wow! You did that!"

HOW GREAT!

The sky isn't always blue! At sunrise and sunset, it turns glorious shades of red and orange, pink and purple. That's because when the Sun is low in the sky, its light has to pass through more of the atmosphere. Those short blue waves get scattered even more—scattering them right out of your sight and letting the longer waves of red and orange shine through.

SAY A LITTLE PRAYER

"Pray like this: Our Father in heaven,
may your name be kept holy."

—MATTHEW 6:9 NLT

You might have seen this holy-looking bug sitting on a tree branch, with its front legs folded up like it's praying. But the praying mantis isn't praying. It's waiting for *prey*. The praying mantis is an *ambush predator*. That means it sits very still, blending in with the leaves and twigs. When a bug, bird, or even lizard or frog happens by, it strikes lightning fast with moves

that would make a ninja jealous! It can even spin in midair, landing right on its target. The mantis seizes its victim with powerful front legs (which are spiked!) and pins it down, often choosing to eat the brains first. *Whew!* Aren't you glad the praying mantis isn't big enough to think *we* look tasty?

The mantis looks like it's praying because that's the way God made it. But He didn't make you to *look* like you're praying. He created you to actually pray. In Matthew 6, Jesus shows you how:

> Our Father in heaven,
>   may your name be kept holy.
> May your Kingdom come soon.
> May your will be done on earth,
>   as it is in heaven.
> Give us today the food we need,
> and forgive us our sins,
>   as we have forgiven those who sin against us.
> And don't let us yield to temptation,
>   but rescue us from the evil one. (vv. 9–13 NLT)

Prayer isn't hard or complicated. No ninja moves are needed. It's focusing on who God is and what He does. It's telling Him what we need and listening for Him to answer—which He will always do.

Lord, thank You for the gift of prayer—and for always listening to me.

EVEN ELEPHANTS HICCUP!

Do not do wrong to a person to pay
him back for doing wrong to you. Or do
not insult someone to pay him back for
insulting you. But ask God to bless that
person. Do this, because you yourselves
were called to receive a blessing.

—1 PETER 3:9 ICB

It's true, even elephants hiccup. So do dogs, lions, and porcupines. (That could get prickly!) Actually, all mammals hiccup. But people do it more often than animals—and babies do it most of all. They hiccup before they're born!

Hiccups happen when the muscle under your lungs, the *diaphragm* (DI-a-fram), jerks suddenly at the same time your vocal cords snap shut—which is what gives the hiccup its . . . well . . . *hic*-cupping sound. Hiccups can happen if you laugh too hard, eat too quickly, or drink a fizzy drink. But hiccups can also be mysterious with no certain cause.

Hiccups can be annoying and occasionally painful, and there's no surefire cure for them. Tricks like holding your breath, eating a spoonful of peanut butter, or breathing into a bag might work—or they might not! Hiccups are just one of those things you can't control.

Like people. You can't control them either. That means sometimes people won't be nice to you. They might annoy you, say terrible things to you, or even bully you. But God doesn't want you to pay back one wrong with another wrong. If someone hurts you, don't hurt them back. Be kind. Pray for that person. Ask for a grown-up's help. And remember: you may not be able to control others or your hiccups, but you *can* control your actions.

Lord, when others are unkind or even mean, help me to remember Jesus and how He loved everyone, even those who hated Him. Then help me to show the same kind of love and kindness to others.

HOW GREAT!

Most hiccups last only a few minutes, but Charles Osborne had a case of the hiccups that lasted from 1922 to 1990. That's 68 years of hiccups! He hiccupped between 20 and 40 times every minute. Doctors estimate he hiccupped more than 430 million times in his life!

BRIGHTER THAN THE SUN

Christ is the visible image of the invisible God.

—COLOSSIANS 1:15 NLT

About 800 light-years away from Earth sits a brilliant star named Rigel (RY-juhl). It's what scientists call a blue supergiant. *Blue* because it burns so hot—twice as hot as the Sun. *Supergiant* because it's, well, gigantic—about 73 times bigger than our Sun. And it's bright. I'm talking *40,000 times brighter* than our Sun! And Rigel puts out about 100,000 times more energy than the Sun. Wait! That doesn't add up! Where did the other 60,000 come from? That energy comes from ultraviolet light, which is invisible. You "see" (ha-ha!), most of Rigel's power is invisible—kind of like our God.

The fact is, no person has ever seen God (John 1:18). In Exodus 33:20, God even said, "You cannot see my face. No one can see me and stay alive" (ICB). Sometimes God would appear in a burning bush or a cloud or as a man or angel—like when He spoke to Abraham and wrestled with Jacob. Moses even once saw God's back as He passed by (Exodus 33:22–23).

You can still know what God "looks" like, though, by looking at Jesus, because He was God in the flesh (John 1:1, 14). Scripture says Jesus is the "visible image of the invisible God" (Colossians 1:15 NLT), and He came to Earth to show us what God is like. The Bible tells us all about Him. Not the color of His eyes or skin, but the important things like His love and kindness, the way He helped people, and how much He loved God, His Father. His character comes shining through, even brighter than Rigel.

Dear God, open my heart to Your Word so that I can see what You really look like. And then please help me to look more like You.

HOW GREAT!

Rigel and the Witch Head Nebula

A light-year is how far light travels in a year, which is 5.88 trillion—or 5,880,000,000,000—miles! Think of it like a space-sized ruler. Light travels fast, speeding across space at 186,000 miles per second. Our own Milky Way galaxy is estimated to be about 100,000 light-years across, but recent studies indicate it may be as wide as 200,000 light-years. Compare that to the Sun, which is "only" about 93,000,000 miles away. That's not even a single light-year!

HOME SWEET HOME

Dear friends, you are like visitors
and strangers in this world.

—1 PETER 2:11 ICB

Animals, even the tiniest ones, build some amazing places to live.
Insects' homes range from apartment-style dwellings to skyscrapers to cozy
little cottages for one. Honeybees like to live together in a big community.
They work together to build their home out of a wax that is made in their own

24

stomachs. The bees chew it and spit it out in such a way that it creates the apartment-style honeycomb they live in. The cathedral termite of Australia also likes to live in communities. It uses clay and sand to build insect skyscrapers that can tower an impressive 26 feet high—that's probably taller than your house! On the other hand, the leaf-rolling grasshopper prefers to live alone. Know where it sleeps? Rolled up in a leaf that it ties shut with a silky thread.

Chewed up wax, sand and clay, rolled up leaves—God gave animals some creative places to call home. Where do you call home? Not just the apartment or house you live in, but where does your heart call home? You may feel like you don't fit in here on Earth, but that's okay! God says that we're just visitors here—and all the sin and evil you see in this world should make you uncomfortable. As God's child, your true home is in heaven, where there will be no sin or pain or sadness. And He's got a place ready just for you.

Lord, thank You for preparing a heavenly home for me. Help me to make this world a better place—one that looks a little more like heaven.

HOW GREAT!

First Peter 2:12 says, "People who do not believe are living all around you. . . . So live good lives" (ICB). How can you help others learn about God—and find their real home in heaven—by living a good life? What can you do today to show someone who God is and how He loves them? Who can you help? It doesn't have to be something big. It just has to be done with love.

O-O-OZONE

Now that I belong to Christ,
I am right with God.
— PHILIPPIANS 3:9 ICB

Ozone is a tiny little gas molecule with a great big job to do. It's sort of a cousin to oxygen—the gas we breathe. But while oxygen is made up of two oxygen atoms stuck together, ozone has three. Ozone has a blue color and an unpleasant smell. In fact, the word *ozone* comes from the Greek word meaning "smelly."

Ozone mostly hangs out in the Earth's upper atmosphere and wraps around our planet like a huge shield. It protects us from the Sun's dangerous, burning ultraviolet rays. Without it, those rays would hit the Earth and cause all kinds of terrible skin and eyes problems—not to mention shriveling up all our plants!

Just as the ozone layer wraps around the Earth, the goodness of Jesus wraps around you and protects you from sin. You see, we all sin. We all do things God doesn't want us to do. Sometimes it's by accident; sometimes it's not. The absolute worst thing about sin is that it "burns up" our relationship with God. But God doesn't want that to happen! That's why He sent Jesus. When you believe that Jesus is the Son of God and you follow Him, His goodness wraps around you—kind of like ozone wrapping around the Earth. It protects you from the terrible effects of sin and makes your relationship with God good again (Isaiah 61:10). Now that's the greatest news of all!

Ozone can also be made when electricity—like lightning—zips through the air. That's why you might notice a strange smell right before or after a thunderstorm. In fact, the world's biggest ozone "factory" is the Catatumbo lightning storm. You can read more about that on page 13.

Lord, wherever I go and whatever I do, I know that You are always with me, watching over and shielding me, helping me to do what's right. Thank You for being my strength and my shield.

27

12

THERE'S A MOON
OUT TONIGHT

God said, "Let there be lights in the sky to
separate day from night. These lights will be
used for signs, seasons, days and years."

— GENESIS 1:14 ICB

The Moon is more than just a big, dusty rock hanging up there in the sky. It gives us ocean waves and 24-hour days. It keeps us from being too hot or too cold. And it makes sure we have just the right amount of Sun. How? *Gravity.* The Moon has gravity. It's not as strong as Earth's, but it does pull on the Earth. It creates *tides*, which are the rise and fall of the oceans that happen each day. The Moon's gravity also slows down the Earth's spin so that our days are 24 hours long—instead of only about six! (Imagine: if days were six hours long, a year would have more than 1,000 days. That's a lot of extra school days!)

The Moon's pull also keeps the Earth tilted in space at a perfect 23.5 degrees. Without the Moon, the Earth might sit straight up, and we'd hardly ever see the Sun. Or it might lay on its side, like Uranus does. Then we'd have 42 years of sunlight followed by 42 years of darkness. Without the Moon, life on Earth would be very different. In fact, there might not even be life at all!

Did you know that the Earth has not just one but two moons? Well, not exactly. Earth's "second moon" is actually an asteroid, but it orbits around the Earth just like the Moon. The asteroid—affectionately called asteroid 2016 HO3—is probably about 120–300 feet in size. It was first spotted by scientists in Hawaii on April 27, 2016.

None of this happened by accident. God placed the Moon in just the right spot to give us perfect conditions for life. All the pieces of God's creation work together, just the way He created them to.

Lord, thank You for the Earth and the Moon and the way You make all things work together. You are amazing!

DON'T SWEAT IT

A foolish person loses his temper. But
a wise person controls his anger.

—PROVERBS 29:11 ICB

On a hot summer day, you've probably noticed this wet stuff dripping down your face. It's called *sweat*, and it's your body's own built-in air conditioner. Sweat comes from the *two to four million* sweat glands you have all over your body. Most of them are on your hands, feet, and face. You see, your body needs to stay at about 98.6 degrees Fahrenheit to keep up its necessary

functions like breathing, digesting food, and making new cells. But when you've been exercising or when it's just plain hot outside, your body can get too hot and make you sick. That's when your brain tells your body it's time to cool off—and the sweat glands get to work, making a watery liquid that gets sent out through the pores (or tiny openings) in your skin. As the sweat evaporates into the air, it cools your skin. Pretty cool, huh?

But our bodies aren't the only thing that can get too hot—our tempers can too! It's so easy for little things to make us angry—whether it's knocking over the milk at lunch, dropping the pencil for the fifteenth time, or getting squirted in the face by the water fountain. But anger doesn't fix the problem. It usually makes it much worse! What can you do to "cool off"? Take a deep breath and say a little prayer. Ask God to cool your temper and simply show you what to do next—like mop up the milk, pick up the pencil *again*, and wipe your face. Learning to let God help you keep your cool during the little stuff makes it easier to keep your cool when the big things come around.

Lord, when little things—and big things—make me want to lose my temper, help me not to sweat it. Remind me to ask You what to do instead.

HOW GREAT!

Want to hear something crazy? Hippos have *pink sweat*! Special glands in their skin put out an oily, reddish-pink liquid that is sometimes called "blood sweat." This sweat isn't for cooling them off though. It's a moisturizer, antibiotic, and sunscreen all rolled into one. As it turns out, hippos have very sensitive skin!

DIVE IN!

I am as happy over your promises as
if I had found a great treasure.

— PSALM 119:162 ICB

A *cenote* (sih-NOH-tee) is a special kind of sinkhole. When the ceiling of an underground cave, well, *caves in*, it creates a sinkhole. If that sinkhole fills up with water—from rain or an underground stream—it becomes a cenote.

The Yucatan Peninsula in Mexico has thousands of cenotes. In fact, most of that area's water comes from them. That explains why they were so

Cenote in Mexico

important to the ancient Mayans who lived there. *Cenote* even comes from an ancient Mayan word that means "sacred well." Today, these pools are often used for swimming and scuba diving. Archaeologists diving into their depths have discovered the fossils of mammoths, sloths, giant jaguars, and even camels, along with pieces of gold, jade, and pottery. And, of course, there are all the natural cave treasures of stalactites and stalagmites. When you dive into a cenote, who knows what treasure you might find!

Kind of like God's Word. When you dive in, you're sure to find a treasure. It might be something about God you never knew before. Or the answer to a tough problem you've been facing. Or a promise that reminds you just how much God loves you. Unlike other books, the words of the Bible are made alive by the power of the Holy Spirit (Hebrews 4:12), which means there's always a treasure waiting for you whenever you dive inside.

Lord, I thank You for the treasure of the Bible. Please teach my heart to want to dive into its treasures every day.

HOW GREAT!

Before you dive into God's Word, say a prayer asking Him to show you the treasure He wants you to find. Then try looking for one of these things: a truth about who God is, a promise God has for you, or an action He wants you to take. Check out 1 John 4:8, Philippians 4:19, and Matthew 22:39 to begin collecting His treasures.

PRETTY IN PINK

Think about the things that are good and
worthy of praise. Think about the things
that are true and honorable and right
and pure and beautiful and respected.

—PHILIPPIANS 4:8 ICB

Have you ever heard the saying, "You are what you eat"? Boy, is that true for flamingos! These beautiful birds are tall, leggy, and . . . *pink!* But believe it or not, flamingos aren't born pink. As babies, their feathers are a light gray color. So what makes them pink? It's what they eat. You see, flamingos eat mostly shrimp and certain kinds of algae that have lots of *beta carotene* (BAY-tuh KAR-uh-teen) in them. Beta carotene is a reddish-orange pigment (the stuff that makes color). Because the flamingos eat so much of it, it colors their feathers! If flamingos were to switch to eating bugs and seeds the way most birds do, their feathers would stop being pink.

Did you know that you are what you eat too? Okay, you probably won't  be turning pink anytime soon, but the things you take in—the things you hear, see, and think about—become part of who you are. For example, it's easy to just sing along to a song without thinking, but do you know what the words are really saying? Would they please God? All those things you watch on TV or those quick little videos on the Internet— would they please God? What about the books you read? Remember, you can never

unsee or unhear something. It will forever be inside your brain, coloring who you are. So be careful what you let in!

Lord, help me to be careful about the things I listen to, watch, and read. Let everything I "take in" be pleasing to You.

HOW GREAT!

Those same beta carotene pigments that make a flamingo's feathers pink can also turn a baby's nose orange! That's right! Beta carotene is also found in carrots, apricots, and sweet potatoes. If babies eat too much of these foods, their noses turn orange—but only until they start eating other foods.

YOU'RE ON THE MOVE!

"Go and make followers of all people in the
world. Baptize them in the name of the
Father and the Son and the Holy Spirit."

—MATTHEW 28:19 NCV

Yep, you're on the move! What's that you say? You're just sitting and reading this book? Well, yes . . . and no. You might *think* you're sitting still, but you're actually riding on a planet that's spinning at about 1,000 miles per hour (give or take a little, depending on where you live). That's faster

than the speed of sound! But that's not all. While you're spinning, this planet—the one we call Earth—is also traveling around the Sun at about 67,000 miles per hour. And at the same time, the Earth, Sun, and our entire solar system are circling around the center of the Milky Way galaxy at roughly 450,000 miles per hour. (Is anyone else feeling a little dizzy yet?)

You are definitely on the move! But God has bigger plans for you than just hurtling through space. He wants your faith to be "on the move" too. Check out what He says in Matthew 28:19: "Go and make followers of all people in the world" (NCV). Then in Mark 16:15, He says, "Go everywhere in the world, and tell the Good News to everyone" (NCV). *Go.* Be on the move. Tell the world about God and how He sent Jesus to save us. Yeah, the world is a pretty big place. But God made you and placed you in just the right spot to be a part of His story. That starts with you and the people you meet every day. So go . . . and tell the world right next to you about your incredible God.

Milky Way galaxy

It takes about 24 hours for the Earth to spin around, or *rotate*, once. It takes about 365 days for the Earth to circle around the Sun. But scientists believe it would take 230 million years for the Earth, Sun, and our solar system to make a loop around the Milky Way galaxy. That trip is called a *cosmic year*.

Lord, I want to go and tell the world about how awesome You are, but it can be a little scary sometimes. Please give me the courage to put my faith "on the move" for You.

STOP AND SMELL THE ROSES

God looked over all he had made, and
he saw that it was very good!

— GENESIS 1:31 NLT

Nothing else smells quite like a rose. But what is it that makes a rose smell so good? It's a little chemical called *rose oxide* (roze AWK-side), which is actually four different chemicals in one. Those four chemicals are arranged in just the right order to give the rose its wonderful "rosy" smell—a little sweet, a little fruity, and a little minty, with just a touch of orangey-lemon. If they were arranged even just a little bit differently, the smell wouldn't be the same.

Scientists will tell you that roses and other plants give off their scent in order to attract insects to fertilize them. But that's not the only reason God made His creation—roses and everything else—so wonderful. God's creation tells us about Him.

The heavens show us how glorious He is (Psalm 19:1). The wonders of nature tell us there must be a Creator (Romans 1:20). And the flowers—so beautiful to see and smell—let us know that God cares about the little things, even the things that bloom today and are gone tomorrow (Matthew 6:28–30).

God's creation praises Him (Psalm 96:11–12). Why not join in? Join the trees in singing for joy (Psalm 96:12). Look at the skies and shout that He is glorious. See the flowers and know He cares about even the littlest things in your life. Go ahead. Put away the phone, the game, and yes, even this book for a few minutes. Step outside and enjoy the wonders of God's creation. Stop and smell that rose—He made it for you.

Lord, thank You for all the little details of this amazing world You have created. Teach me to see something wonderful in it every time I open my eyes.

HOW GREAT!

The saying "a rose by any other name would smell as sweet" comes from William Shakespeare's play *Romeo and Juliet*. It means something is special because of what it is, not what it is called. So what other names does a rose get called? Well, it's *rosa* (ROH-zuh) in Italian, *méiguī* (MAY-gwee) in Chinese, and *bara* (bah-RAH) in Japanese.

THE BEST MEDICINE

A happy heart is like good medicine.

— PROVERBS 17:22 ICB

Whether you giggle, tee-hee, or guffaw, laughter is one language that everybody speaks. You don't have to learn to laugh either. It's a skill you're born with. Babies start to laugh when they're only about three months old—long before they learn to say *mama* or *dada*.

Real laughter is one of those things that just happens. Something seems funny, and before you can even think *That's funny*, your brain has you laughing. But you can't *make* yourself really laugh. (Go ahead, give it a try.) Laughter is also contagious. If you hear someone laughing, chances are, you'll soon be laughing too. Some people even claim laughter can heal you—like medicine. Scientists aren't sure about that, but we do know that laughter is fun, helps you make friends, and makes you feel good inside.

Laughter is a gift from God. It heals our heart and gives us joy. God even tells us there is a time to laugh (Ecclesiastes 3:4). But there's a huge difference between laughing *with* someone and laughing *at* someone. Don't use laughter like a weapon to hurt others or to tear them down. Always try to treat others the way you want them to treat you (Luke 6:31)—and nobody likes to be laughed at! Laughter is a gift, and it's meant to be shared. A funny story and a good laugh might be just the medicine a friend needs during a tough day. Remember, words and actions—yes, even laughter—should always be loving and kind . . . and that's nothing to joke about!

Lord, thank You for the gift of laughter. Help me to use it in a way that makes You smile and brings the joy You've given me to others.

HOW GREAT!

There's nothing like a tickle fight to get the laughter and giggles going. But here's a question: Can you tickle yourself? As it turns out, the answer is no. A big part of the reason you laugh when tickled is because you're surprised. If you try to tickle yourself, your brain knows what's coming. You're not surprised, so you're not tickled!

SPRING, SUMMER, FALL, AND WINTER

Everything on earth has its special season.

—ECCLESIASTES 3:1 ICB

Spring and summer, fall and winter—you know what the seasons are, but have you ever wondered *why* we have them? It's because the Earth doesn't sit straight up and down in space. It tilts, or leans, a little—23.5 degrees, to be exact. So as the Earth makes its 365-day trip around the Sun, the amount of sunlight that falls on each part of the Earth changes a little bit every day. The places that get more sunlight have summer and spring while the places that get less sunlight have fall and winter. Because the Earth is always moving, the seasons are always changing. When it's freezing cold during the winter, you can know the summer sunshine is on its way! In fact, it's already happening somewhere on Earth!

The seasons aren't the only things that are constantly changing. In fact, just about everything on this Earth is changing. Families change, schools and jobs change, friends change—even you change! Sometimes it can be hard to know what you can count on because everything seems to be changing! But remember this: God never changes. Nope. Not ever. He's the same today as He was yesterday, and He'll be the same tomorrow too (Hebrews 13:8; James 1:17). So when He says He loves you (John 3:16) and He'll always be there for you (Matthew 28:20; Deuteronomy 31:6), you know it's true— spring or summer, fall or winter. Seasons come and go, but God always stays the same.

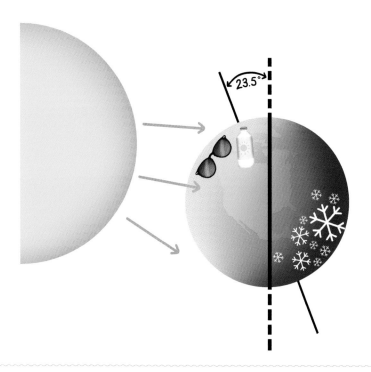

Lord, no matter what "season" I'm in—whether it's sunshiny or sad or somewhere in between—I know that You have a purpose for it. Help me to trust You.

HOW GREAT!

Did you know that when it's summer in North America it's winter in Australia? That's because for half the year the top half of the Earth (or *Northern Hemisphere*) is tilted more toward the Sun, so it has the warmer seasons of spring and summer. At the same time, the bottom half (or *Southern Hemisphere*) is tilted away from the Sun, giving it fall and winter. For the other half of the year, the Earth tilts the opposite way—so the seasons are reversed!

POWER IT UP!

Yours, O Lᴏʀᴅ, is the greatness, the power, the
glory, the victory, and the majesty. Everything
in the heavens and on earth is yours.

—1 CHRONICLES 29:11 ɴʟᴛ

When you hear the word *power*, you may think of a king, someone who has the power to rule over and control others. Or you might think of a weightlifter who has the power to lift heavy weights. Or you might even think of the electricity that powers everything from lightbulbs to smart

phones. But in the science of physics, power means something different. Power describes how fast you use energy. For example, it takes the same amount of energy to *walk* across a football field as it does to *run* across a football field. But running is faster. Therefore, running has more power. This is the kind of power that makes things happen.

No matter what kind of power you're talking about, God has it all. He's the ruler of this universe and able to control everything in it—from the stars to the storms. He's got the power to move mountains, oceans, and galaxies. He created the power of lightning and can hold it in His hands (Job 36:32). As for the power to make things happen, no one is greater at that than our God. And what's the greatest thing He makes happen? A way to heaven. We can't get there on our own power. But with the power of God we can!

Lord, no one is more powerful than You. Thank You for pouring Your power into my life—to help me live the way I should and to make a way for me to get to heaven.

HOW GREAT!

Have you ever heard the word *horsepower*? It's used to describe how powerful a machine is, especially a car. This measurement was first created back in the 1700s by Isaac Watt. He wanted to help farmers understand just how powerful his steam engine was compared to the power of a horse. One horsepower is the amount of power needed to move 550 pounds one foot in one second. The average NASCAR racecar has around 800 to 1,000 horsepower.

PRETTY POISON

There is no truth in [the Devil]. When he
tells a lie, he shows what he is really like,
because he is a liar and the father of lies.

— JOHN 8:44 NCV

With its bright orange and black wings, the monarch butterfly is
so pretty and so . . . *poisonous*? Well, at least it is for the birds and lizards
looking to make a meal of it.

HOW GREAT!

Adult monarchs lay their eggs on the poisonous milkweed plant. The eggs hatch into caterpillars, which eat the plant. But instead of killing the caterpillars, the poison becomes part of their body, even when they transform into butterflies. So any bird looking for a quick and colorful snack gets a nasty surprise. The poison doesn't kill the bird, but it does make it sick. Because monarchs are so easy to recognize, birds quickly learn not to eat them.

Monarchs aren't the only pretty things that turn out to be poisonous. Sin can be pretty poisonous too. That's because Satan likes to dress sin up in pretty colors to try to trick you into giving it a try. For example, Satan might disguise a lie as an easy way to get what you want. Or he'll try to make breaking a rule look like just having fun with your friends. Or he'll try to make a bad movie look like it will make you laugh. He might even make drugs look like a way to fit in. But lies lead to more lies, and breaking rules leads to broken friendships. That movie that looks so funny can plant yucky words and thoughts in your head. And drugs? They can tear up your whole life! So before you try that pretty thing that looks so good, talk to God about it. Ask Him to show you if it's really poison in disguise.

Hands down, the deadliest creature on land or sea is the sea wasp jellyfish. Its body can grow to the size of a basketball, but its tentacles are 10 to 15 feet long—and there are 60 of them. Each one is covered with stinging cells. Sea wasps simply swim along, waiting for prey to get trapped in their tentacles. If a person were to get tangled in those tentacles, they could die in just four minutes!

Dear God, teach me to see things as they really are and not to be tricked by Satan's poisons in disguise.

47

OVER THE RAINBOW . . . MOUNTAINS?

The Lord your God is God. He is the
faithful God. He will keep his agreement
of love for a thousand lifetimes.

—DEUTERONOMY 7:9 ICB

When you see the Rainbow Mountains of China, you just might think you're dreaming. But don't pinch yourself! These colorfully striped mountains are completely real.

They were formed when different layers of sandstone and minerals were pressed together under the ground—and then pushed above ground when the *tectonic* (tek-TON-ik) plates under the Earth's surface shifted. The rainbow colors were created when the different minerals inside the sandstone touched the air and *oxidized* (AWK-si-dized), or rusted—just like how your bike will rust if you leave it outside too long. Different minerals "rusted" to different colors, giving us the Rainbow Mountains!

Those rainbow-colored mountains might remind you of another rainbow: the one God first gave to Noah. Do you know the story? People had grown so wicked that no one even thought about goodness or God anymore. Except Noah. Noah truly loved God. So when God sent a flood to destroy the sinful living creatures who filled the Earth,

A *moonbow* is like a rainbow, except that it is created by the Moon's light rather than the Sun's light. Moonbows are very rare. When they do appear, it's often near a waterfall. Moonbows can be seen at Cumberland Falls in Kentucky and Victoria Falls in Africa when the Moon is full.

He saved Noah and his family. After the waters dried up, God promised never to flood the whole Earth again. And He gave Noah a sign of His promise: the rainbow. Now, whenever you see a rainbow—in the sky or in a mountain—you can remember not just God's promise to Noah but *all* His promises. Because they're your promises too. And God will keep every single one of them. That's how great our God is!

Dear God, the colors of this world are amazing to see. But even more amazing are all Your promises to me—and I know You will keep every single one.

THE MEDULLA WHAT?

Jesus has the power of God. His
power has given us everything we
need to live and to serve God.

—2 PETER 1:3 ICB

The *medulla oblongata* (muh-DOO-la ah-blon-GAH-tuh) is fun to
say, but it's also very important. It's the part of your brain that sits right
on top of your spinal cord, and it acts sort of like a messenger service. You

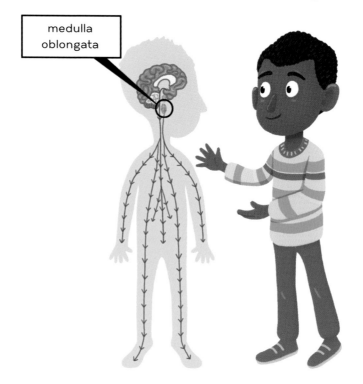

medulla
oblongata

see, your brain sends out messages to tell the rest of your body what to do. At the same time, your spinal cord sends messages back to the brain, telling it what the body is up to. All those messages are passed back and forth by the medulla.

The medulla also controls your heartbeat, blood pressure, and breathing. These are called your *autonomic functions*—the stuff your body does without thinking. Imagine having to tell your heart to beat every time. Or your lungs to breathe in, out, then in again. The medulla takes cares of all that for you—even things like coughing, sneezing, and swallowing.

Have you ever stopped to think about all the things God takes care of for you? Like giving you air to breathe and the Sun to wake up to each morning. When you stop to count your blessings, do you count the blessing of fingers to count on? Or of knowing how to count? Or of having a voice to count with? The greatness of God and His gifts are all around you—remember to thank Him for every one!

Dear God, You have blessed me in more ways than I can count! Show me something new to thank You for each day.

HOW GREAT!

You've heard the saying "Count your blessings." And you've probably made lists of all the things you're thankful for. This time, try something a little different. Make a list of God's gifts to you—and include at least one thing you can't see, one thing you use all the time, and one thing you've never thought to thank God for before.

SAY IT ISN'T SO

Lord God, you are God, and
your words are true.

—2 SAMUEL 7:28 ICB

Elephants drink water through their trunks like a straw. Bats are as blind as a, well, bat. An ostrich hides by sticking its head in the sand. Touching a toad will give you warts. Bulls will charge at the color red.

How many of these "facts" have you heard? As it turns out, they aren't true! Here are the real facts: Elephants suck water only part of the way up their trunk and then pour it into their mouths. Bats mostly use sound to navigate,

but they can also see. Ostriches don't stick their heads in the sand, though they might flop on the ground and play dead. No, you won't get warts by touching a toad. And bulls *will* charge at the color red, along with blue, green, yellow—any color at all, if it's moving.

We hear some things so often that we start to think they must be true. But the thing is, this world—and the Devil who roams around in it—likes to lie. It says things over and over again, like *You aren't important, No one really cares about you, You're not good enough,* or *You've got to face your troubles all by yourself.* Don't believe it! Arm yourself with God's truths by reading the Bible every day. You'll learn how special you are, how much you're loved, and how you're never alone. Then you won't be tempted to believe the lies.

Lord, I hear so many different things about who I am and who You are. Help me remember to always check Your Word for the truth. I know You'll never lie to me.

OUT OF THIS WORLD

God sits on his throne above the circle of the earth.
And compared to him, people are like grasshoppers.
He stretches out the skies like a piece of cloth.
He spreads them out like a tent to sit under.

—ISAIAH 40:22 ICB

Have you ever wondered what it would be like to be an astronaut?
Space is very different from Earth, so living in space is very different too. First
of all, there's no air in space, so astronauts have to take oxygen with them in
their spacecrafts. To work outside in space, they must put on a special suit.

There's also no gravity in space, so astronauts are weightless—they float! That sounds fun, but on Earth gravity helps us know which way is up. In space astronauts can't know if they're standing straight up or sideways or even upside down! That can really play some tricks on the tummy—kind of like riding on a rollercoaster. Even catching some shut-eye is a different experience. When astronauts sleep in space, they have to tie themselves to something so they don't float around!

There's no air or gravity in space, but do you know what there is? God. He's here on Earth and there in space and everywhere in between. His presence fills the farthest corner of the universe as well as the corner of your heart, all at the same time. God's great that way. What does that mean for you? It means that whenever you're feeling upside down—whether you're on a rollercoaster, in a spaceship, or in a really uncomfortable situation and not sure what to do—God is right there with you. Tie yourself to Him. He'll show you which way is up, which way to go, and what to do.

God, my mind just can't think big enough thoughts to describe how great You are. You made me, You made this Earth, and You made every star in space. You are amazing!

HOW GREAT!

Astronauts get to eat all kinds of different foods, from macaroni and cheese to freeze-dried ice cream. But there are a few things they can't have—like cookies, crackers, and bread. Why? Because the crumbs would end up floating around and getting into equipment or the astronauts' eyes. So astronauts eat tortillas instead! They do get to have salt and pepper, but it's in a liquid form.

26

RAIN OR SHINE

"Your Father causes the sun to rise on
good people and on bad people. Your
Father sends rain to those who do
good and to those who do wrong."

— MATTHEW 5:45 ICB

Extreme. It means that something is about as far from ordinary as you can
get. Like deserts and rainforests.

Deserts get less than 10 inches of rainfall a year. Hollywood movies show

deserts as being hot and dry, with mile after mile of sand dunes—and sometimes they are. But deserts can also be rocky—or even icy and cold, like the deserts in the Antarctic and the North Pole.

Rainforests, on the other hand, get more than 75 inches of rain a year. Now, you're probably thinking of tropical rainforests like the Amazon, but there are rainforests all over the world in places like Asia, Australia, and the United States. Rainforests are usually hot and humid—and filled with all kinds of plant and animal life.

Deserts and rainforests are extreme, but life can be extreme too. Some days are like being in a rainforest where you're showered with good things. Other days feel more like a desert, without a drop of happiness in sight! And when you're having a "desert" day, it's *really* hard to understand why that kid who was so mean to you is getting showered with good things. But remember this: God loves every person, even those who

Taylor Dry Valley in Antarctica

The village of Mawsynram in India has the honor of being the wettest place in the world. It gets an average of more than 467 inches of rain every year! But the Dry Valleys in Antarctica are—you guessed it—the driest place on Earth, with an average annual rainfall of *zero*!

don't love Him back. Blessings might be His way of getting their attention so that they'll learn to believe in Him. As for your "desert" days, God promises to use them for your good (Roman 8:28)—and that's a pretty great blessing.

Lord, I don't understand why bad things happen to good people and good things happen to bad people. But I do know You love me and You are always blessing me—rain or shine.

THE GOOD FRUIT

Live a life worthy of the Lord and please him
in every way: bearing fruit in every good
work, growing in the knowledge of God.

— COLOSSIANS 1:10 NIV

We think of fruit as being yummy and good for us, but what is it really? Well, fruit is formed from the flower of a plant. It acts like a kind of seed holder. The fruit covers the seeds and protects them until they're ready to grow into a new plant.

When you hear the word *fruit*, you probably think of the kind that grows on trees. And many fruits do, including apples, oranges, and peaches. But fruits like watermelon, cantaloupe, and grapes grow on vines, while others—like raspberries and strawberries—grow on bushes or small plants.

And then there are the fruits that grow in your life. Okay, so they aren't the kind of fruits you eat. Instead, they're the kind that grow out of your heart. If your heart doesn't have the love of Jesus in it, the fruits will be bad—like anger, selfishness, and hate. But if your heart is full of Jesus' love, the fruits will be good. They'll include the fruit of the Spirit that Galatians 5:22–23 talks about. And your fruit will overflow into good works. Want to know if you're growing good fruit? Ask yourself these questions: Did you help someone today? Do you look a little bit more like Jesus today than you did yesterday? Are you helping others look more like Jesus? If you can say yes, then you're growing some great fruit!

Lord, fill up my heart with Jesus so my life will overflow with Your good fruits!

HOW GREAT!

When you think of summertime, you might think about biting into a sweet strawberry. This delightful fruit is grown in every one of the 50 US states and all 10 Canadian provinces. But its name is a little misleading: strawberries aren't technically berries since they wear their 200 seeds on the outside of their skin. Nonetheless, this amazingly delicious fruit has its very own museum in Belgium called The Strawberry Museum.

THE AMAZING ANTEATER

Lord, help me control my tongue. Help
me be careful about what I say.

—PSALM 141:3 ICB

Guess what an anteater eats. What? How did you know? Yes, an anteater eats ants—and sometimes termites. But mostly ants. There are different types of anteaters, but the most well-known is the giant anteater. It lives in Central and South America and can grow to about seven feet long. But as big as it is, the anteater has a tiny mouth—only about an inch or so wide.

The anteater has really sharp claws to rip open anthills and rotting wood to get to the bugs inside. But what's really amazing is its tongue. Long and thin like spaghetti, an anteater's tongue can be more than two feet long—the longest of any animal. The anteater can flick that tongue in and out of its mouth up to 160 times a minute! It's sticky too—helping it to slurp up as many as 30,000 ants and termites every day!

An anteater can do a lot of damage with that tongue. And while your tongue may not be two feet long, it can also do a lot of damage—to the people around you. That's why the Bible says we should be quick to listen and slow to speak (James 1:19). It's important to think about what you're going to say before you say it. Before you speak, try this little test: Are your words true? Are they helpful? Are they kind? If they aren't, it's a good time to give your tongue a rest!

Lord, help me remember to think before I speak so that the things I say honor You and those around me.

HOW GREAT!

Anteaters are amazing swimmers. They use their long snout like a snorkel! And their four-inch-long, sharp claws not only make great digging tools but also help defend the anteaters against cougars and jaguars.

CYCLING AROUND

We are workers together for God.

—1 CORINTHIANS 3:9 ICB

You've heard of bicycles, motorcycles, and even unicycles, but have you heard of the *water cycle*? No, it's not a bike made for water. (But wouldn't that be fun?)

The water cycle is the way water moves around the Earth. It's like a gigantic circle—without any real beginning or end. Liquid water is stored in oceans, rivers, streams, and even mud puddles. When the Sun heats the water's surface, the water travels up to the sky as vapor. That's called *evaporation*. The vapor cools into tiny water droplets. This is called *condensation*. Water droplets gather together to make clouds, which then send the water back to Earth as rain, snow, sleet, or hail. That's called *precipitation*. Precipitation waters plants and gathers in oceans, rivers, and streams. Then the cycle starts all over again.

Water in all its forms is so very important. We need liquid water to drink, vapor to form clouds, and ice to keep our planet at just the right temperature. Every form of water has a job to do, kind of like we do as children of God. We all have important jobs to do for God. Some of those jobs look different, but they're all so important (1 Corinthians 12:12–27). And the cool thing is that God will give you everything you need to do the job He has for you (Hebrews 13:20–21). If He wants you to be an encourager, He'll give you a tender heart—and people who need encouraging. If He wants you to help someone, He'll give you the strength and courage to do it. And if He wants you to be a writer, He'll give you words. How great is that?

Dear God, thank You for the unique way You made me and the gifts You've given me. Help me to use them to show the world who You are.

HOW GREAT!

When you take a sip from the water fountain, do you ever think about how *old* that water you're drinking is? Because the water cycle is the ultimate example of recycling, that water could have been sipped by George Washington or even splashed in by a dinosaur!

30

THAT'S AMAZING!

With God's power working in us,
God can do much, much more than
anything we can ask or imagine.

— EPHESIANS 3:20 NCV

In 2013, Tiny Meeker set a world record on the bench press, lifting 1,102 pounds. That's the same weight as a bison! Athletes must train their bodies to do amazing things. But your body does some completely amazing stuff each and every day:

- Your nose can remember about a trillion different smells.
- Your heart beats about 100,000 times every day and 36,500,000 times every year.
- Your body is made up of trillions of cells, and each one has its own job to do.
- Your nerves send messages to your brain at a speed of about 250 miles per hour—and racecars go only about 200 miles per hour!

Jesus said that the most important of all commands is this: "Love the Lord your God. Love him with all your heart, all your soul, all your strength, and all your mind" (Luke 10:27 ICB). Your challenge today (and every day!) is to show your love for God in all four ways. How can you love Him with your heart, praise Him with your soul, serve Him with your hands and feet, and learn something about Him with your mind?

God gave your body some pretty spectacular abilities. And I think He did that so you would know just how powerful and creative He is. But all these incredible things your body can do are just the beginning! The most powerful stuff happens inside your heart. When you decide to follow God, He gets to work in your life, helping you do more than you could ever imagine. Tough stuff like loving grumpy people and forgiving others. Helpful stuff like serving. And the really great stuff like telling others about Him.

But God doesn't just work *powerfully* in your life; He also works *creatively*. That means the way you love and serve and share about God can look *completely* different from the way someone else does. Whether it's through singing, painting, baking cookies, or raking a neighbor's leaves—or any of a million other ways—God will help you use your life to show the people around you just how much He loves them. God is just that great!

Lord, You are so great, and You've given me this amazing body. Show me how to use my hands, my feet, my brain, and my heart and soul to serve You. Help me reflect Your power to the watching world!

31

A WHOLE NEW YOU!

If anyone belongs to Christ, then he
is made new. The old things have
gone; everything is made new!

—2 CORINTHIANS 5:17 ICB

Take a look at your hand. It's not just holding this book. It's actually very busy making new skin cells. The top layer of your skin—the part you see—is called the *epidermis* (eh-pih-DUR-mis), and it's made up of skin cells. Lots and lots of them. Scientists think you have about 1.6 trillion skin cells throughout your body, depending on how big you are, of course. New skin cells are constantly being made at the bottom of your epidermis. They move up to the top of your epidermis in a trip that takes about a month. When they reach the top, they quickly die and fall away. In fact, you lose about 30,000 to 40,000 dead skin cells every minute. So in the time it's taken you to read this paragraph, you've probably lost about 35,000 skin cells already. Don't worry! Your body replaces the dead cells with new skin cells just as fast. No wonder you're tired!

Your skin isn't the only part of you that God is making new. When you decide to follow Him, God takes your heart, your mind, and your spirit and begins making them new too. It doesn't happen all at once—or even in a month. It's a change that happens your whole life through. But each day God helps you get rid of your old, "dead," selfish ways. He teaches you to be more like Jesus instead, sharing God's love and joy with everyone around you.

God, please help me shed my old selfish ways. Help me to be more like Jesus instead.

HOW GREAT!

Every year you lose about eight pounds of dead skin cells. Where do they go? Well, you know all that dust on your bookshelves and tables and pictures? That's mostly made up of dead skin cells! You might say that you leave a little bit of yourself wherever you go!

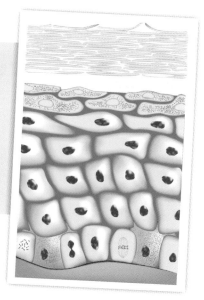

67

PUT 'EM UP

The Lord will fight for you.

—EXODUS 14:14 NIV

Plants have enemies of many shapes and sizes—from tiny bugs that like to nibble away their leaves to bigger animals that eat the whole leaf or plant!

But plants can't exactly run away from danger, so how do they defend themselves? Some plants have tiny, fur-like prickles on their leaves that help keep insects away. Others—like the rose—have thorns, which are basically extra-sharp twigs. Still others, like the cactus, have larger spikes called *spines* that keep bigger animals away.

Then there are other plants that use a chemical defense system. Their leaves might look tasty, but one bite and—*blech!*—animals find them too bitter to eat. Or they might be poisonous. Some even put out a sticky sap that traps and kills any bug that tries to eat them. Plants might not be able to throw a punch or karate chop an enemy, but God still gave them ways to fight off their enemies.

You have an enemy too—the Devil. He prowls around like a roaring lion, looking for someone to eat (1 Peter 5:8). He'd like nothing better than to chow down on your hope, tear away your faith, and shred your love for God. But just like plants, God doesn't leave you defenseless. In fact, God promises that He will fight for you! All you need to do is stand up to the Devil by trusting God—and the Devil will run away from you (James 4:7).

God, I know the Devil is real and that he wants me to turn away from You. But I am going to trust You to fight for me and keep me safe from his evil. Thank You for the promise of Your protection!

HoW GREAT!

It's a cute little plant with a silly-sounding name—but look out! Australia's gympie-gympie is nothing to joke about. Tiny little hairs cover its heart-shaped leaves and stick into anyone unlucky enough to touch this plant. Victims says it feels like being electrocuted and hit with hot acid—all at the same time! In fact, its poison is so powerful that 100-year-old dried leaves can still sting!

33

MAGNETOSPHERE IS HERE!

You can trust God. He will not let you be
tempted more than you can stand. But
when you are tempted, God will also give
you a way to escape that temptation.

—1 CORINTHIANS 10:13 ICB

Magnetosphere. It sounds like a comic book superhero, doesn't it? Well, in its own way the magnetosphere *is* a hero, shielding us from the dangers of the Sun.

You see, the Sun doesn't just give out light and heat. It also shoots out bits of electrically charged matter at a speed of about 1 million miles per hour! This is called *solar wind*. The magnetosphere is like a huge, magnetic bubble that wraps around the Earth and traps those bits of matter. Without it the solar wind would hit our atmosphere at full force. Over time our atmosphere would wear away, and we'd be hit with all the Sun's ultraviolet radiation. There wouldn't be enough sunscreen in the world to protect us, which wouldn't matter because there wouldn't be any life left on Earth to protect! The magnetosphere is just one of the amazing ways God takes care of us.

Solar winds aren't the only dangers we need protection from. There will be days when temptations come toward you like a blast of solar wind. Maybe you start to think, *Everyone else cheats on tests,* or *No one will ever know,* or *It's just a little lie.* Without protection temptations can wear you down. But God promises to wrap you in His bubble of protection. Talk to Him and tell Him what's tempting you. When temptation tries to trap you, God promises to help you escape.

Lord, I'm amazed by the way You protect us from dangers we don't even see. I pray that You will protect me from temptations—the ones I see and the ones I don't see.

HOW GREAT!

Did you know that the Earth is actually a gigantic magnet? Yep! And the North Pole and South Poles are the most magnetic, while the equator is the least. Many kinds of animals are able to sense that magnetism and use it to help them navigate. Some, like the blind mole rat, use it to help them know which direction is which. Others, like monarch butterflies and whales, use it to travel long distances.

Blind mole rat

34

JUST FOLLOWING THE CROWD

God is the One I am trying to please. . . .
If I wanted to please men, I would
not be a servant of Christ.

— GALATIANS 1:10 ICB

We've all felt it. That pressure to follow the crowd, to fit in, to do what everyone else is doing. It's called *peer pressure*. And we humans aren't the only

ones who feel it. Some animals do too. South African monkeys will switch the foods they eat when they switch to a new group—even if they didn't like that food before. In a group of whales in New England, one whale started smacking its tail on the water before it gathered up fish to eat. Soon several other whales copied its tail-smacking ways. Brown rats and chimpanzees will also follow the crowd when trying to figure out how to get treats.

It's natural to want to fit in. Sometimes it's okay to go along with the crowd, but sometimes it isn't. Like when you feel pressured to do something you don't want to do. (No, cleaning your room doesn't count!) Or when others want you to do something you know is wrong or even dangerous. Whether it's making fun of someone just because everyone else is or trying alcohol or a drug, there are times when you need to stand up to the crowd and say no. You're trying to please God—not the kids on your team or the cool kids at school. God wants you to be like Jesus, not like everyone else. And who knows, when you stand up and do what's right, someone just might copy *you*!

Dear God, help me to think less about pleasing people and more about pleasing You. Help me follow You even when it's not the popular thing to do.

HOW GREAT!

You've probably played a game or two of follow-the-leader, but you've never played it quite like this! On November 10, 2015, in Salt Lake City, Utah, 768 people joined together to play the world's largest game of follow-the-leader. Imagine being at the end of that line!

35

A ONE AND A TWO . . .

You are great, and you do
miracles. Only you are God.

—PSALM 86:10 ICB

Living here on Earth, we tend to think of the Sun as a pretty extraordinary star. But the truth is, compared to other stars, our Sun is quite ordinary. And that's a good thing! Our Sun is steady, sure, and consistent—letting off the perfect amount of light and heat. But one thing makes our Sun unique, and that's the fact that there is only one.

You see, most of the stars you see in the night sky aren't just one star— they're actually two stars circling each other. Scientists call them *binary stars*. (Remember, *bi* means "two," just like in *bicycle*.) About 80 to 85 percent of all stars are binary. But our Sun is *nonbinary*, which means there's only one. And that's a very good thing for us! If there were two suns in our sky, we'd have double the heat and double the dangerous UV rays. Life on Earth wouldn't just be unpleasant; it would be downright impossible!

Just as there is only one Sun in our sky, there's only one God in the whole entire universe. Throughout history, people have created all sorts of gods for themselves—from Baal to Zeus—but not one of them is real. And none of them can do what the one true God can do. Only He could set the stars in their places—the binary and the nonbinary ones. Only He could tell the Sun how much to shine. And only He could create you. No god created by man could ever be greater than our God!

Lord, only You are God. There is no other god who can do all the great and mighty things You can do. Teach me to love You with all my heart.

HOW GREAT!

Just as there is only one God, there is only one way to get to Him. What is that way? Find the answer in John 14:6.

NAILED IT!

Do all that you can to live in
peace with everyone.

— ROMANS 12:18 NLT

Fingernails. They're good for scratching an itch and scraping off sticky price tags. But there's more to those nails than you might think!

The part you see is called the *nail plate*. It's mostly made up of dead cells. The pink color you see comes from all the blood vessels underneath. Your nail

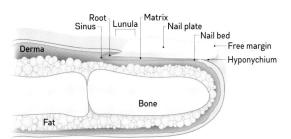

grows out of the *nail root*, which is under your skin. See that white, half-moon shape at the base of your thumbnail? That's called the *lunula*, and it's the end of the nail root. Your nails grow as new cells push the older cells toward the end of your finger. Fingernails protect the tips of your fingers (and toenails protect your toes).

Though nails have an important purpose, they are also responsible for one of the most horrifying sounds known to mankind—fingernails scratching across a chalkboard. *Aaahhh!* Scientists have found that this sound causes your body to feel actual physical stress. Plus, it's just so annoying!

Some people make sounds just as annoying as fingernails on a chalkboard. Make sure you aren't one of them! Don't whine and complain when you're asked to do something or if you have to wait in a long line. If you've had a bad day, don't take it out on your friends. And don't argue with your brother or sister just because you're bored. Try to "live in peace with everyone"—then you won't be like fingernails on a chalkboard.

Lord, help me to be pleasing to You in all I do and say. And help me to think of others before I think of myself.

HOW GREAT!

Have you ever noticed that you have to trim your fingernails a lot more often than your toenails? That's because your fingernails grow two to three times faster than your toenails. Fingernails grow about one millimeter (that's about as thick as a paperclip) every 10 days or so. But toenails take a month to grow that much!

IT'S ALL IN THE ADVERTISING

"No one lights a lamp and then puts it under a basket. Instead, a lamp is placed on a stand, where it gives light to everyone in the house."

—MATTHEW 5:15 NLT

If you've ever touched a butterfly's wings, you've probably gotten some powdery dust on your fingers. What is that stuff? It's not dust. It's

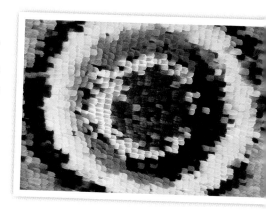

scales! A butterfly's wing is covered with tiny scales that overlap each other, like the shingles on a roof.

What are those scales for? Well, the darker colors soak up the Sun's warmth and help the butterfly get warm enough to fly. (Did you know butterflies are cold-blooded?) But one of the main reasons for those brightly colored patterns of scales is advertising. That's right! Just like on TV—except these advertisements are a warning. They say to would-be predators, "You don't want to eat me. I taste *really* bad!"

God created butterflies to advertise who they really are—yucky-tasting bugs. And He created you to do the same thing. You were created to advertise who *you* really are—a follower of Jesus. So . . . do you? Do your friends know you're a Christian? Do your neighbors know you love Jesus? Can the people who live in your house tell that you're trying to be more like Jesus? Don't hide your love for God—advertise. Tell the whole world how great you think He is!

Lord, I want to tell the world how amazing You are. Show me how I can advertise Your greatness today!

HOW GREAT!

Butterflies may look dainty and delicate, but they're pretty tough travelers! The monarch butterfly travels up to 2,750 miles from Canada to Mexico in its migration to warmer winter climates. But the painted lady butterfly flies even farther—about 4,000 miles from North Africa to Iceland, all while flapping its wings about 20 times per second!

38

CREATED TO SHINE

The sun has one kind of beauty. The moon has
another beauty, and the stars have another.
And each star is different in its beauty.

—1 CORINTHIANS 15:41 ICB

Pollux (POL-uhks) is a funny-sounding name for a very bright
star. It's located more than 33 light-years away from Earth. (Just one light-
year is almost 6 trillion miles, so Pollux is really, *really* far away!) This star is

what scientists call a *red giant*. *Giant* because it's so huge—about 10 times bigger than our Sun. It even has its own planet orbiting around it. And *red* because it is slowly burning itself up, giving off a reddish-orange light. But Pollux is perhaps best known for the way it shines—more than 30 times brighter than our Sun. For thousands of years, sailors have used this bright, shining star to guide them.

God created Pollux to shine. It doesn't shine quite the same way as the Moon or the Sun, but it is still beautiful in its own way, just like everything God created—especially you. Now, there may be something about you that you think isn't so beautiful or purposeful. But try to think of it this way: God created you on purpose, just the way He wanted you, from your head down to your toes. And then He stepped back and said, "Magnificent! Fantastic! *Beautiful!*" You are beautiful in your own fearfully, wonderfully, made-by-God way. And just like Pollux, God created you to shine.

Just as Pollux's bright light guides sailors on their way, you can guide others on their way to Jesus. How? Be kind when others aren't. Be helpful when it isn't easy. Do the right thing when others don't. And when people ask you why you're so different, you can tell them about the One you are following.

God, teach me to see the beauty that You have created all around me. And especially help me to see the beauty that You have created in me.

39

NOT-SO-SOLID GROUND

Truly he is my rock and my salvation; he
is my fortress, I will never be shaken.

—PSALM 62:2 NIV

The ground we stand on isn't quite as solid as it seems. And in certain places around the world, it can suddenly disappear!

You see, the ground beneath our feet is made up of dirt, rocks, and minerals. Water from rain and underground streams constantly seeps in and slowly wears away—or *erodes*—the rocks and minerals. Over time it can wash away the underground bedrock support that holds up the surface land. That's when the ground caves in and a hole appears—a *sinkhole*. A sinkhole can form slowly over time—or in an instant. Some are only a couple of feet across, but others are more than 2,000 feet wide. Sinkholes occur more frequently in places where the bedrock is a weak material that easily dissolves or erodes. Builders in places that are prone to sinkholes have to be careful about where they build. They need to be sure they're building on a solid foundation.

Like a builder, you must be careful about what you build your life on—what your foundation is. Do you depend on your money? Because it can be

stolen. Do you depend on your smarts? Sooner or later, there'll be a question you can't answer. Do you depend on friends? What if they move away? Money, smarts, and friends can be good things, but they're all things that can shift and change—leaving you in a hole! Build your life on God. Depend on Him. He never shifts or changes. And He'll never leave you in a hole!

HOW GREAT!

Sometimes sinkholes can pop up—or cave in—in the most unexpected places, like the National Corvette Museum in Kentucky. In 2014, early in the morning, a sinkhole suddenly opened up inside the museum and swallowed eight Corvettes! The sinkhole has been repaired, but the cave remains. Visitors can look through a window to see the floor of the sinkhole, more than 30 feet below.

Dear God, You never shift or change like the things of this world. I know I can always count on You!

A JOYFUL NOISE

Come, let us sing for joy to the LORD; let us
shout aloud to the Rock of our salvation.

— PSALM 95:1 NIV

Are birds born knowing how to sing? Actually, no. Unlike cats that are
born knowing how to meow and dogs that know how to bark, birds have to

learn their songs. They learn by listening to their mom, dad, and other birds. And it takes *a lot* of practice. Some of their songs are pretty complicated!

So why do birds sing? It's not really for conversation. Birds use single "words," or *calls*, for things like warning other birds of danger, telling where to find food, and simply saying hello. But when it comes to their full songs, it turns out birds sing for a lot of reasons! If you hear a bird singing in North America and Europe, it's probably a boy bird—and he's usually singing to impress a girl (or maybe warn another guy to stay away). But if you live in Australia or the tropics, that bird you hear singing is probably a girl, and she's usually putting on a show. But sometimes birds sing when they're all alone. Why? Scientists think it's for the same reason we do—just for the pure joy of singing.

God has given you so many things to be thankful for—the wonders of His creation, the blessings of people who love you, the beauty

The mockingbird is known for its singing. The male mockingbird sings more often than the female and can make up to 200 different noises. It's called a mockingbird for its ability to "mock" or imitate other sounds— from the songs and chirps of other birds to a cat's meow to a car alarm!

of birdsong. It's enough to fill your heart with song, so why not sing out a few praises? Don't worry about how you sound or if the notes are just right. Sing just for the pure joy of praising the One who gives you so many reasons to sing.

Lord, put a new song in my heart and mouth today—a song of praise to You!

LEFT, RIGHT . . . LEFT?

If you go the wrong way—to the right or to the left—you will hear a voice behind you. It will say, "This is the right way. You should go this way."

—ISAIAH 30:21 ICB

Raise your hand if you're left-handed. Chances are not many of you would. That's because only about 10 percent of the world's population is left-handed. (That means people use their left hand for things like writing and throwing a ball.) And scientists don't really know why. Some think it has to do with your DNA—that blueprint inside your cells that makes you, *you*. Others think it has to do with the way the left and right sides of your brain develop when you're a baby.

Most people are able to use only one hand—either the right or the left—for things like writing. Some are able to write with one hand and throw a ball with the other. And very few, only about 1 percent, are able to use both hands equally well. Those people are called *ambidextrous* (am-bi-DEK-struhs).

When it comes to choosing which hand to use, you probably don't have to think about it. It just comes naturally. But other choices are tougher—like what to do about a problem. That's when you should talk to God. Tell Him what the trouble is. Yes, He already knows, but talking about it can help you sort it out together. God promises that if you need help, He'll show you what to do—through the Bible or through another person. Whether it's to the right or the left, God will keep you headed the right way.

Lord, remind me to talk to You about all the choices I need to make. I trust You to show me the right way to go!

HOW GREAT!

The saying about walking in someone else's shoes means trying to understand how someone else feels. So many of the things we use every day—from scissors to spiral notebooks to your computer mouse—are made for right-handed people. Try being left-handed for a day. Write, eat, and throw a ball with your left hand. Or if you're left-handed, try using your right! Whether it's battling a spiral notebook or finding a baseball glove that fits, trying to understand how others live will make you a more thoughtful, kind, and loving person—just like Jesus wants you to be!

TYPHOONS, HURRICANES, AND CYCLONES . . . OH MY!

"I have called you by name, and you are mine."

—ISAIAH 43:1 ICB

Typhoons, hurricanes, cyclones . . . what's the difference? Location, location, location! These are actually three different names for one kind of

storm—a *tropical cyclone*. In the Atlantic Ocean this kind of storm is called a *hurricane*. In the South Pacific it's a *cyclone*. And in the western Pacific it's a *typhoon*.

No matter what you call it, tropical cyclones are powerful. Their winds start at about 74 miles per hour but can speed up to well over 150 miles per hour. They send waves crashing against the shore, and the really strong ones can rip out trees and flatten buildings. Tropical cyclones can stretch from 60 to more than 1,200 miles across, and they can contain the power of hundreds of thunderstorms!

It's hard to even imagine that kind of power. But the power of a tropical cyclone is nothing compared to the power of our God. All He had to do was say the word, and light shot out across the universe, stars appeared in the sky, waters gathered into oceans, mountains moved into place, lions roared to life, and people walked on the Earth. Then He said, "It is finished," and sins were washed away, death was defeated, and Satan lost forever (John 19:30 ICB). *That* is power. And that is the God who loves you and calls you by name.

Lord, You are so huge and so powerful. You can do absolutely anything—and You still know my name. I just love that about You.

HOW GREAT!

In the Southern Hemisphere (the half of the planet south of the equator), cyclones spin clockwise, just like the hands of a clock. But in the Northern Hemisphere (north of the equator), cyclones spin *counterclockwise*, the opposite of the way the hands on a clock spin. This is called the Coriolis effect, and it's caused by the earth's rotation. Some people say it even affects the way water spins in a toilet bowl—but that's just a myth!

TO THE EXTREMES!

I pray that the God of peace will give
you every good thing you need so
that you can do what he wants.

— HEBREWS 13:20 ICB

God filled our planet with amazing animals and equipped them to live in some of the most extreme climates on Earth. Like the Himalayan jumping spider. This eight-legged wonder lives some 22,000 feet up in the Himalayan mountains. Its home is three-fourths of the way up the tallest point on earth—Mount Everest. It survives by eating bugs blown up the mountain by the wind. On the other side of the world, the giant kangaroo rat (which is only about a foot long) doesn't even need to drink water—a good thing since it lives in Death Valley, one of the driest places on Earth. It gets the liquid it needs from the seeds it eats. Then there's the *Paralvinella sulfincola*. Don't worry. I can't say it either. Just call him Mr. Worm. He's a cute little guy with a feather-duster face who lives near underwater vents that reach up to 170 degrees Fahrenheit! The wood frog goes to the other extreme. In winter this little hopper hides under fallen leaves. A natural antifreeze chemical in its body keeps it from freezing to death.

From mountaintops to sea bottom, and from desert heat to winter forests, God created animals to survive—even thrive—wherever He places them. And He does the same thing for you. In fact, Psalm 139:3 says God already knows every path you'll ever walk, every place you'll ever be, every problem you'll ever face. So you can trust Him to know—and give you—everything you need to not only survive but thrive!

Dear God, thank You for making a way for me. No matter where I am or what I face, I know You'll equip me with everything I need to thrive!

HOW GREAT!

The Afar people of Dallol, Ethiopia, live in one of the hottest places on Earth—on top of an active volcano where temperatures can reach as high as 145 degrees Fahrenheit! As nomads, they survive by moving mostly at night, eating lots of salt to replace the minerals they sweat out, and drinking milk. Yep, milk! Scientist say it's as hydrating as any sports drink.

THE LITTLE THINGS

"If you are faithful in little things, you
will be faithful in large ones."

— LUKE 16:10 NLT

While it might not be the prettiest flower you'll ever see, the *Wolffia globosa* (WULF-fee-uh glob-OH-suh) holds the record for being the tiniest. How tiny? You know those yummy candy sprinkles on your cupcake? *That* tiny! The Wolffia is a water plant that's found all over the world, and the entire plant is only about one millimeter long. If you were to gather up a bouquet of a dozen Wolffia flowers, they would all fit on the head of a pin. Five thousand would fit in an ordinary thimble. And do you see this letter *O*? Two whole Wolffia plants could squeeze inside it. Now that's tiny!

Little things are important to God, from these little flowers to all the little things you do. You see, when you help a friend pick up the books she dropped, choose to be kind to the cafeteria worker at school, or help that kindergartner tie his shoe, it might not seem like a big deal to you—but it is to that friend, that cafeteria worker, and that kindergartner who doesn't have to worry about losing his shoe! And it's a big deal to God. When you choose to do what's right in the "little things" of life, God will give you the chance to do what's right in the really big things too!

Lord, thank You for always keeping Your promises to me. Please help me to be faithful too—in big and little things.

HOW GREAT!

Wolffia globosa may be tiny, but it still serves a big purpose. You see, it also goes by the name *duckweed*, and it's a tasty treat for—you guessed it—ducks, along with other birds and fish. Scientists are even looking into ways to harvest it for pigs, chickens, and cows to eat. Umm . . . yum?

JUST GLOW WITH IT!

My God brightens the darkness around me.

—PSALM 18:28 ICB

Has this ever happened to you? You climb into bed and turn off the lights. But instead of darkness, an eerie green glow shines from across the room. Your heart thumps and you can barely breathe . . . until you remember it's the glow-in-the-dark stickers you slapped on your backpack. *Whew!*

What makes something glow in the dark? It's these cool little things called *phosphors* (FOS-fers), which soak up the sunlight as energy. Over time they slowly release that energy as light. That's the glow you see. Toymakers mix phosphors into the plastic they use to make glow-in-the-dark toys, stickers, and other stuff. Glow sticks work a little differently. They glow when two chemicals mix together—that's why you have to "snap" the stick. Whether it's from a phosphor or from two chemicals mixing together, even a little glow can chase away the darkness in your room.

But rooms aren't the only things that can be dark. Sometimes your days can be dark with sadness, fear, and worry. That's when you need the "glow" of God to brighten it up. Sadness is no match for the brightness of His joy. Fears flee from His courage. And when worries shadow you, His love sends them running. Your God doesn't just "glow" in the darkness. He chases it away.

Did you know some animals glow in the dark? It's true! The anglerfish (perhaps one of the ugliest creatures on Earth) lives up to a mile deep in the ocean. Sprouting from its head, like a fishing pole, is a thin rod with glowing bait on the end. Other fish see the light, think it's something to eat, and swim right into the angler's mouth!

Dear God, when my world starts to look dark, remind me to talk to You and to let Your love light up my life. I trust that You are always in control of my life!

46

CHANGING THE STARS

God is working in you to help you
want to do what pleases him. Then
he gives you the power to do it.

—PHILIPPIANS 2:13 ICB

About 37 light-years away from Earth is a star called Arcturus (ark-TOO-ruhs). It is a red giant star that scientists believe is nearly 25 times the size of our Sun. Arcturus is one of the brightest stars that we can see in our night sky. It is so bright that it shines 115 times more light than our Sun. But

Arcturus is changing. As it slowly burns up its outer layers, it is being changed into a much, much smaller white dwarf star.

Now think about this: If God can change a star that is 25 times bigger than our Sun (and our Sun is so huge it would hold more than 1 million Earths), just imagine what He can do with you! Because as awesome as changing a star is, the change that God is working inside you is even more amazing.

God is like a potter, and you are His lump of clay—a very precious and wonderful lump of clay. Each day He shapes and changes you. He uses His Word, the people around you, and the things that happen in your life to teach you to do what pleases Him. Like doing what's right when you just want to pretend nothing is wrong. And being brave when you'd rather hide. And having peace even though everything seems to be going wrong. God is changing you to be like Jesus—and that's the greatest change of all.

Dear Lord, change isn't always easy or fun. But I trust You to change me and make me more like Jesus.

HOW GREAT!

On a clear night, if you look up into the sky, you can find a group of stars called the Big Dipper. Look for three stars in a row—they form a sort of curved handle. Then look for four more stars off to the side—they form a sort of bowl. The "bowl" together with the "handle" make up the Big Dipper. Now imagine that that curved handle just kept curving on around—that curve will lead you right to Arcturus!

47

ON THE TRAIL

Live a life of love. Love other people
just as Christ loved us. Christ gave
himself for us—he was a sweet-smelling
offering and sacrifice to God.

—EPHESIANS 5:2 ICB

With its droopy ears, sad puppy-dog eyes, deeply wrinkled skin, and drooling mouth, the bloodhound doesn't exactly look like an ace detective. But this four-legged crime fighter is the best in the business—the tracking business, that is.

Police departments have used the bloodhound to track down criminals and lost or missing people for nearly 200 years. That's because God made this dog to be a master sniffer. For starters, its sense of smell is about 1,000 times stronger than ours. And those long, droopy ears aren't just for show. They sweep along the ground and funnel scents up to its nose! Even all that wrinkly skin works to trap scents. A bloodhound can follow a scent trail that's 300 hundred hours old—that's almost 13 days! Even with all the technology we've invented, nothing is as great at tracking as the bloodhound God made.

Did you know that the kind of life you live also leaves a trail? It's not a scent trail that a bloodhound would follow. But it should be a trail that leads others—not just back to you but to God. How? By leaving a trail of kindness wherever you go. Don't stink up your "scent trail" with gossip, hurtful words, or selfishness. Leave the sweet smell of love everywhere you go.

Lord, help me not to stink up this world with angry words or selfishness. Instead, let me leave the sweet scent of love and kindness wherever I go.

HOW GREAT!

How does a bloodhound track a person? First, it sniffs something the person has worn, like a shirt or hat. This gives the dog an *odor image*—a sort of "smelly picture"—to follow. The bloodhound's nose is so powerful that it can find that smelly picture in the jumble of all the other smells in the world and follow it. Bloodhounds have been known to follow a trail for more than 130 miles!

48

DON'T BE FOOLED!

Beg for understanding. Search for it
as you would for silver. Hunt for it like
hidden treasure. Then you will understand
what it means to respect the Lord.
Then you will begin to know God.

—PROVERBS 2:3–5 ICB

Have you ever heard of the California Gold Rush? It happened between 1848 and 1855, when rumors of gold had more than 300,000 miners rushing to the western United States. The earliest miners panned for gold. That means they would scoop up dirt, gravel, and water—often from a stream or riverbed—and shake it back and forth in a pan. The heavier gold would settle to the bottom where the miner could pick it out. A few did strike it rich, but others were fooled by a shiny, worthless mineral called *pyrite* (PY-rite)—or *fool's gold*.

Fool's gold looks like what you *think* real gold should look like—shiny and golden. But real gold is actually kind of dull looking. Real gold is also pretty soft. If you hit it with a hammer, it will flatten out. If you hit fool's gold with a hammer, it'll give off sparks. Real gold has no smell, but fool's gold really stinks—like rotten eggs. Many miners thought they had found great treasure when all they had was a shiny, stinky, worthless hunk of rock.

That sounds like a lot of the "treasures" people chase in this world. Worldly treasures sparkle and shine—it's so tempting to rush after them. But when you compare them to *real* treasure, they're stinky and worthless. What's the real treasure? Knowing God! He's the greatest treasure of all. God is the only thing worth rushing after. And He's so much easier to find than gold. Just open up your Bible and open up your heart in prayer. The greatest treasure of all—God—is right there, just waiting to be found.

Dear God, when I'm tempted to rush after the treasures of this world, help me to remember that You are the greatest of all treasures. I want to spend my whole life getting to know You.

Pyrite

HOW GREAT!

The California Gold Rush is the most famous in America, but it wasn't the first. The Carolina Gold Rush began in 1799 when a 12-year-old boy discovered a 17-pound gold nugget. More than 30,000 people rushed to the area to begin searching for gold. Carolina then led the nation in gold production every year after that—until 1848, that is!

Gold

49

EXCUSE ME!

Confess your sins to each other
and pray for each other.

— JAMES 5:16 NLT

Burp. Belch. Or—for the scientific types—*eructation* (e-RUHK-tay-shun). It happens to us all about 6 to 20 times a day. What makes us burp? Air. You see, when you eat or drink, chew gum, or even talk too fast, you swallow air. All that air builds up in your tummy until your body pushes it out with a rumbling *buuurrrppp*. Eating too fast or drinking fizzy sodas (which are full of tiny gas bubbles) makes you burp even more.

Humans aren't the only ones who burp. Animals do too. In fact, cows burp so much that if you could somehow collect a year's worth of burps from just 10 cows, you'd have enough gas to heat a house for an entire year!

Most people think it's rude to burp. So if one slips out, you should say, "Excuse me!" It's a way of apologizing for what you did. But burping isn't the only time you should apologize. Any time you realize you have hurt or offended someone—accidentally or on purpose—it's a good idea to say you're sorry. Ask that person to forgive you, and try not to make the same mistake again. And if you do something that hurts or offends God (that's called *sin*, by the way), you should do the same thing. Tell God you know what you did was wrong, say you're sorry, and ask Him to forgive you. He always will (1 John 1:9)!

Lord, when I do things that hurt others, help my heart to be ready to say I'm sorry. And when I do things that hurt You, help my heart to be ready to apologize to You too. Teach me to honor You with my actions.

HOW GREAT!

The record for the longest burp is 1 minute, 13 seconds, and 57 milliseconds. It was "achieved" by Michele Forgione of Italy in 2009. But the record for the loudest burp belongs to Paul Hunn of the United Kingdom. His burp was 109.9 decibels—that's louder than a motorcycle!

50

BLIND AS A . . . WORM?

For we are God's masterpiece. He has created us anew in Christ Jesus, so we can do the good things he planned for us long ago.

—EPHESIANS 2:10 NLT

If you've ever stepped outside after a rain shower, you've probably seen a bunch of earthworms slithering along, hurrying to get back underground. Why the rush? Because earthworms breathe through their skin. If their skin dries out, they'll die! (There's also the danger of birds looking for a quick snack.) And with no arms and no legs, getting underground is hard work. Special bands of muscles push the earthworm forward. Tiny bristles on its body grip the soil, and a slippery mucus coating helps it slide through the dirt. The earthworm doesn't have any eyes either, but it *is* able to sense light, especially with its front end, which helps it move away from the Sun.

Even with no arms, legs, or eyes, the earthworm plays an important part in our world. By churning up the soil, it moves nutrients to the top and creates holes that let in air and water.

If an earthworm can do all that, just imagine what you can do with the arms, legs, and eyes God gave you! You can use your eyes not only to see the wonders and goodness of His creation but also to see the people around you who are hurting or in need. Your arms can reach out to give a hug and to help someone who has fallen. And those legs God gave you are great for going—to serve others and to tell them about Him.

Dear Lord, teach me to use my arms, my legs, my eyes—my whole body—to show the world how great You are!

HOW GREAT!

Most earthworms are only a few inches long, but the Australian Gippsland earthworm averages around three feet in length and can grow to more than 10 feet long. They're so big that they can sometimes be heard gurgling as they burrow under the ground!

Earthworm

51

LET'S DEW IT!

"For I am about to do something new. See, I
have already begun! Do you not see it? I will
make a pathway through the wilderness. I
will create rivers in the dry wasteland."

—ISAIAH 43:19 NLT

Have you ever stepped outside in the morning when the grass,
leaves, and even the spider webs seemed to sparkle with a thousand little diamonds? It didn't rain, so what is that stuff? It's dew!

When temperatures cool during the night, the water vapor in the air *condenses*, or forms into tiny drops of water that fall on everything. (If the temperatures dip down below freezing, those drops will freeze into tiny crystals called *frost*.) But dew isn't just pretty; it can be a lifesaver in places that don't get a lot of rain. Plants, animals, and even people capture dew to use it for water. Dew is just one of the amazing mechanisms God created to take care of this world and His people.

Sometimes God uses miraculous ways to take care of us. For example, when the Israelites escaped from Egypt and were wandering in the desert, there wasn't much food to be found. So God made a way for His people to get food. Each morning as the dew dried, thin flakes of bread appeared and covered the ground. The people called it *manna*, and it tasted sweet like honey. Psalm 78:25 called it "the bread of angels" because it came from heaven (ICB). (You can read more about manna in Exodus 16.) It's just one of the amazing ways God takes care of His people. You can always trust that wherever God leads you, He'll provide the perfect care for you.

HOW GREAT!

You've heard of basking in the Sun, right? Well, in the Namib Desert of Africa, the darkling beetle is all about basking in the *fog*. When the fog rolls in, the beetle sticks its rear end in the air. Bumps and grooves on its wings collect water from the foggy air and funnel it right into its mouth.

Lord, I am so amazed by all the different ways You take care of this world and the people in it. But most of all, I'm so grateful for the way You take care of me!

52

CLOSER THAN YOU THINK

The Lord himself will go before you. He
will be with you. He will not leave you or
forget you. Don't be afraid. Don't worry.

— DEUTERONOMY 31:8 ICB

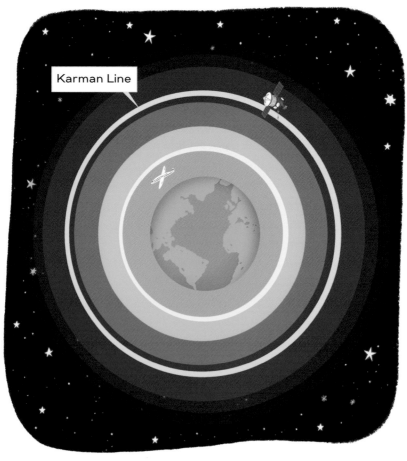

Karman Line

When you look up at the stars, space seems so far away. And while it's not like walking to your neighbor's house, it's closer than you think. In fact, in 2018, scientists started to think that it's even closer than *they* think! Scientifically speaking, space begins where Earth's atmosphere ends—at a point called the Karman Line. For years, scientists believed that line was about 62 miles away. Now they think it might be only about 50 miles away, which means that if you could drive a car straight up, you'd be in space in less than an hour! Space might seem impossibly far away, but it's really quite near.

Like God. There will be times when He feels far away. Perhaps it's when you're hurting or sad, worried or afraid. Or when you've done something you know is wrong. But God is always right there with you. That's a promise He gives over and over again throughout the Bible. When Joshua faced a terrible battle, God promised to be with him wherever he went (Joshua 1:9). When Jesus was about to leave His disciples and return to heaven, He said, "I will be with you always" (Matthew 28:20 NCV). God even says He will pick you up and carry you close to His heart (Isaiah 40:11).

God's not far away. He's much closer than space. He's in your heart, right by your side every moment of every day. What a great promise!

God, because I can't see You with my eyes, it sometimes feels like You're very far away. Help me to "see" with my heart and mind and soul that You are always right here with me.

When you're worried or scared or having a not-so-great day, sometimes a giggle can help chase the blues away.

What kind of songs do the planets sing? *Neptunes!*

Why did the Sun go to school? *To get brighter!*

What is an astronaut's favorite key on the keyboard? *The space bar!*

53

I'M OUTTA HERE!

When you are tempted, God will also give
you a way to escape that temptation.

—1 CORINTHIANS 10:13 ICB

Imagine you're a cute little lizard basking in the Sun and hoping a juicy bug will wander your way—when suddenly, a bird swoops in out of nowhere. You try to run, but it grabs your tail, thinking you'd make a tasty meal! What's a lizard to do? Drop your tail and run!

That's right! Some lizards, like the anole lizard, can just drop their tail and leave it wriggling on the ground. This distracts the bird (or other predator) long enough for the lizard to escape. Pretty cool, huh? Scientists call this *autotomy*, which is a scientific way of saying, "I'm outta here!" Then the lizard spends the next 60 days growing a new tail.

There'll be times when you need to practice a little autotomy too. No, not dropping your tail—after all, you don't have a tail to drop! But when temptation tries to catch you, ask God to help you say, "I'm outta here!" Like when a friend tries to get you to lie, to cheat on a test, or to hide something from your parents. Or when watching that TV show you like tempts you to say things you know you shouldn't say. The fact is, you're going to be tempted in this world. Trust God to help you be strong and to say, "I'm outta here!" when sin tempts you.

Lord, help me know when I need to "drop everything" to get away from temptation.

HOW GREAT!

Did you know that a deer's antlers are *deciduous* (dih-SIJ-oo-uhs)? That means they fall off and are regrown every year. Some species of deer can regrow antlers weighing as much as 60 pounds in only about three to four months!

54

GOD BLESS YOU!

When you talk, you should always be
kind and wise. Then you will be able to
answer everyone in the way you should.

— COLOSSIANS 4:6 ICB

ACHOO! That's the universal sound for a sneeze. Sneezing—or *sternutation*
(stur-new-TEY-shun)—is your body's way of getting rid of something that's
irritating your nose. You might sneeze because you have a cold. Or because

dust, pet hair, or pollen is tickling inside your nose. Some people even sneeze when they step out into the sunlight!

When something irritates your nose, special nerves send a message to your brain. (Fun fact: you can't sneeze when you're asleep, because those nerves are asleep too.) Your brain then tells all your body parts to work together to sneeze—from your chest and tummy muscles to your throat and eyelids. When you sneeze, as many as 100,000 little droplets shoot out your nose at 100 miles per hour, traveling 20 feet or more. So please—cover your sneeze with a tissue or your sleeve!

Sneezes travel pretty far and fast, but there's something else you've experienced that travels faster and farther: *gossip*. Gossip is spreading rumors. It's saying hurtful things about someone—things that may not even be true! And some people do it for fun. But the Bible has a lot to say about gossip, and none of it is good. God says gossip is a sin, just like lying, fighting, and murder (Romans 1:29). So don't spread hurtful words. Share helpful words instead!

Dear God, please help me control my words. Help me be careful about what I say. Let me only say things that are good and helpful and kind.

HOW GREAT!

In the United States people often say the phrase *Bless you* or *God bless you* after someone sneezes. But in Germany they say *Gesundheit*, and in Italy it's *Salute*. Both words mean "health." In Nigeria, in the Igbo language, they say *ndo*, which means "sorry." But in Korea, they don't say a thing!

55

HELLOO-OO-OO!

What were the earth's foundations
set on? Or who put its cornerstone in
place? Who did all this while the morning
stars sang together? Who did this
while the angels shouted with joy?

— JOB 38:6-7 ICB

Stepping inside even a small cave is like stepping into another world. Now imagine a cave so big it has its own lake, river, waterfall, and even jungle! That's what you'll find when you step inside the Hang Son Doong

(hahng-shun-dwong) cave in Vietnam. At more than 5.5 miles long, it's the world's largest known cave. Some of its chambers are so big that you could fit an entire city block inside—complete with 40-story skyscrapers! One cavern is so huge that a Boeing 747 airplane could fly right through. Just imagine the echo in there! And in places where the roof has caved in, sunlight streams down on prehistoric-looking jungles growing some 600 feet below the surface of the Earth!

But perhaps most amazing is the fact that no one even knew about this wonder until 1991 when a local man just stumbled upon it. Then even he couldn't find it again for almost 20 years! God had made all that wonder and beauty, and no one knew about it!

The creativity of our God is endless. No matter how much you learn about Him and this world He has created, there will *always* be something new for you to discover. And if God did all that inside a hidden cave, just imagine the wonder and beauty He has created inside you!

Hang Son Doong

Hang Son Doong might be the biggest cave, but the longest is Mammoth Cave in Kentucky. More than 400 miles have been explored so far, but new caverns are being discovered all the time. No one knows how far this cave goes—except God, of course!

Lord, the things You have created on this Earth just amaze me! A cave big enough to fly an airplane through? Wow! I can't wait to see what You create in me and in my life.

HOW DO THEY KNOW?

Ever since the world was created, people have
seen the earth and sky. Through everything
God made, they can clearly see his invisible
qualities—his eternal power and divine nature.
So they have no excuse for not knowing God.

—ROMANS 1:20 NLT

Animals are born just knowing how to do certain things. These are
called *instincts*. They're like built-in knowledge for how to survive. For example,
just-hatched sea turtles *instinctively* head for the ocean—and they know how

to swim when they get there! Bees *instinctively* take care of their beehive and make honey. Butterflies *instinctively* lay their eggs on just the right kind of plants. Spiders spin their webs, and birds build nests—all because of instincts.

Some people say that different animal species just developed their instincts over time. But the truth is this: God created the creatures of the sea and birds of the air and all the animals that roam the land with exactly the instincts they need to survive in the world. Why? To point us to Him. Because it's impossible to look at just one animal with all its instincts and think, *That just happened.* You see, God wants each and every one of us to know that He is real, that He loves us more than we could ever understand, and that He sent His Son, Jesus, to make a way for us to live with Him in heaven forever. But how could God get us to see all that? How could He get us to see how much He loves us? By showing us how He cares for His creation. Those turtles *know* which way the water is, those bees *know* how to make honey, and those birds *know* how to build the nests they need—all so that you can *know* there is a God who will always love and take care of you.

Lord, when I look at the animals of this world—the spiders that spin their webs, the birds that build nests, the turtles that swim—I just **know** *You are real. Thank You for the examples of Your glory throughout the world.*

HOW GREAT!

Every animal has some sort of instinct, even humans—at least when we're babies. Babies instinctively cry when they are hungry or hurting. And if you put your finger or a toy in a baby's hand, she will instinctively grab hold!

THE SPICE OF LIFE

Let the teaching of Christ live in you richly.

— COLOSSIANS 3:16 ICB

Do you like to eat spicy foods? While lots of different kinds of spices are used in our foods, the pepper is one of the most popular.

You might be surprised to learn that peppers are a fruit. They're a cousin of the tomato, which, yes, is also a fruit. But they're not related to the ground black pepper on your dinner table. That's a completely different kind of

plant—though it's a fruit too. (In fact, ground pepper comes from a berry called a *pepper-corn*. It's cooked and dried and then ground into the powder we call pepper.)

Peppers come in all shapes, sizes, and colors—and levels of hotness. The bell pepper is sweet, while chili and jalapeño peppers are much hotter. Peppers can be eaten by themselves, raw or cooked. Some are dried and ground into spices like paprika. Others are chopped up and added to other foods. Some people even like to add a little chili pepper to their hot chocolate! However you choose to use it, pepper adds flavor to your food.

Food is never dull or boring when there's pepper around. Just as you flavor your food with pepper, you can flavor your life with the Word of God. It's never dull or boring. There has never been a more exciting book written. It's full of action and adventure, heroes and villains, and the greatest love story of all time—God's love for you. Go ahead! Spice up your life with the Word.

> *Lord, thank You for the Bible, for its stories, the examples of how I should live, and—most of all—for its promises from You to me.*

Carolina Reaper

To measure how hot a pepper is, scientists use a scale called the Scoville Heat Unit. A sweet bell pepper has a Scoville rating of 0 units, while a jalapeño rates at 2,500 to 8,000 units. The hottest known pepper (so far!) is the Carolina Reaper at 1,641,000 units. That's 200 times hotter than a jalapeño! Taking a bite out of that one can be dangerous—even deadly!

STUCK LIKE GLUE

All of you should live together in peace.
Try to understand each other. Love each
other as brothers. Be kind and humble.

—1 PETER 3:8 ICB

What do you think? Is coral a rock or a plant? Actually, it's an animal. And that piece of coral you see is made up of hundreds, even thousands, of individual corals called *polyps* (POL-ips) all living together. The polyp itself is soft. It takes calcium from the seawater and uses it to make a hard, outer skeleton around itself. As thousands of polyps join together, they form the outer skeleton that gives coral its rocky appearance.

In addition to all those polyps living together, reefs of coral are home to hundreds—even thousands—of different creatures. The coral offers them shelter, food, and places to lay their eggs. Coral reefs even act like nurseries for larger fish, keeping their babies safe until they're big enough to travel the ocean on their own.

Coral survives, and helps other creatures survive, because all those little polyps stick together. Just like we, as God's children, should stick together. In the Bible this is called *unity*. But since we don't actually *stick* together like polyps, what does unity mean? First Peter 3:8 gives us some clues. It means we put ourselves in other people's shoes and try to understand what they're thinking and feeling. It's being kind and humble—not thinking we're better than anyone else. And most of all, it means we love each other in good times and tough times, *especially* when we disagree. Because when we stick together, we can do great things for our great God.

Lord, teach me how to live and work with all those who love You. Together, we can do great things—like working together to tell even more people about You!

HOW GREAT!

Australia is home to the world's largest coral reef: the Great Barrier Reef. It's made up of at least 2,900 smaller reefs and stretches more than 1,600 miles across. It's so huge that astronauts can see it from outer space!

HOW COOL IS THAT?

Holy, holy, holy is the LORD Almighty;
the whole earth is full of his glory.

—ISAIAH 6:3 NIV

Just outside the town of Juneau, Alaska, you'll find mile after mile of glaciers. One is called Mendenhall Glacier, and it's more than 12 miles long. The outside looks like every other glacier, but hidden inside is a beautiful secret. To find it, you'll have to paddle your kayak across Mendenhall Lake (or hike across if it's winter). Then you'll climb down the ice into the glacier itself,

so be ready to slip and slide! Once inside, you'll discover the magical beauty of the Mendenhall Ice Caves.

These *ice caves*, or *glacier caves*, were carved out by melted glacier water. They're constantly changing as the water freezes, melts, and refreezes. And unlike the blinding bright white of the outside glacier, these caves are a brilliant "glacier blue." Standing inside one feels more like standing inside a watery, frozen aquarium than an underground cave. Who could have dreamed such beauty would be found *inside* a giant, frozen hunk of ice?

Mendenhall Ice Cave

The beauty of God is not only extraordinary but is in the most unlikely of places. It's inside every single person—yes, even that hard-to-get-along-with person you don't like so much. You might have to search for it. You might have to kayak across a lake of bad attitudes or climb a glacier of grumpiness. But when you're willing to search and when you're guided by God's love, you'll find His beauty inside every heart. Yep, even that one.

Dear God, thank You for the amazing beauty I can see all around me. And please teach me to search for the beauty in others that I don't always see.

HOW GREAT!

Did you know that almost 10 percent of the Earth is covered by glaciers? But those glaciers store about 75 percent of the world's water supply!

RUNNING OUT OF FUEL

"Come to me, all of you who are weary and
carry heavy burdens, and I will give you rest."

— MATTHEW 11:28 NLT

If you look up at the night sky, you might notice a reddish-looking light and think it's Mars, the Red Planet. It might be—or it just might be a star called Antares (an-TAR-eez). Antares is a red supergiant that's about 700 times bigger than the Sun. It's also more than 10,000 times brighter.

Antares region of the Milky Way galaxy

Antares is surrounded by a huge cloud of reddish metallic dust, which is why it sometimes gets mistaken for Mars.

The other interesting thing about Antares is that scientists think it will one day explode in a supernova (which is what the explosion of a star is called). It will explode because it's running out of the fuel—or the gases—it burns. (Remember, stars are basically great big balls of burning gases).

Do you ever feel like that? That you'll explode because you're running out of fuel? Maybe you've run out of patience and your anger is about to explode. Maybe you've had one problem after another, and you just can't take it anymore. Or maybe you've just been so busy keeping up with school, family, friends, chores, and practices that you're ready to drop. When you feel like you're running out of fuel, don't explode. Run to God and let Him give you rest. Not just sleep—though that's important too. God will give you rest from worrying and trying to figure everything out on your own. He'll give you the fuel you need to keep going, to keep doing what's right, and to keep following Him.

Lord, when I get too busy, remind me to stop and spend time with You.

HOW GREAT!

How can you be refueled by God? Slip away for some quiet time alone to read His Word, say a prayer, or sing a song of praise. Or simply curl up and fall asleep—and let the Lord who loves you keep watch over you.

A STICKY SITUATION

God showed his great love for us by sending
Christ to die for us while we were still sinners.

—ROMANS 5:8 NLT

In September 2018, the town of Aitoliko, Greece, looked like something out of a scary movie. A massive spider web blanketed part of the town. It was more than 1,000 feet long and was filled with thousands of spiders. *UGH!* That gigantic web was actually spun by a spider that's less than an inch long—along with a few million of its buddies. The reason for the web? Hot and wet weather, along with an especially big population of tasty gnats, made Aitoliko the perfect spot for spiders and turned the town into one big spider party complete with refreshments. But this party left grass, trees, street signs—basically anything that wasn't moving—covered with a thick, sticky web. Fortunately, the spiders weren't dangerous, and the blanket of web only "stuck around" until the weather cooled and the gnats disappeared.

While that blanket of spider webs might not top your wish list, there's another kind of blanket that will. It's the blanket of God's love. You can't see it, but it covers you completely. And unlike spider webs that disappear with a change in the weather or touch of a duster, God's love sticks around no matter what you do. There's nothing so terrible you can do that it will make Him take His love away. And there's nothing you have to do to earn His love. It's yours to keep—no sticky strings attached.

Thank You, God, for the warmth of Your love. It covers me better than any blanket ever could!

HOW GREAT!

It's raining . . . *spiders?* It doesn't happen very often, but when it does, it's amazing to see. In Australia, millions of tiny spiders climb to the highest point they can (like a fence post or plant stalk), release a bit of web that

acts like a sort of parachute, and launch themselves into the wind. Australians call it *spider rain*, while scientists call it *ballooning*. Spider rain can also happen in Great Britain and the United States.

THE EYEBROWS HAVE IT

Your happiness will show in your eyes.

— PROVERBS 15:30 ICB

Thin and light, or thick and bushy, eyebrows aren't just for looks. Practically speaking, eyebrows keep water and sweat from falling into your eyes. But they're also great for talking. Yes, *talking*! Think of all the things you can say with your eyebrows. Both eyebrows raised up high tells the world you're surprised. One raised brow says you're suspicious or don't quite believe what someone is telling you. Both eyebrows lowered and all scrunched together says you're probably angry, annoyed, or confused.

When you say something without saying a word—like raising your eyebrows to show surprise—that's called *nonverbal communication*. The fact is, you can have a whole conversation using just your face, body, and actions without ever opening your mouth. For example, if you're walking toward someone, what are you "saying" when you smile? What about when you frown? Or when you pretend you don't even see them? First Timothy 4:12 says you should be an example to others in the way you speak—and that includes the conversations you have without saying a word! Make sure your face shows kindness with a smile. Show people they're important to you by looking them in the eye—and that you respect them by not rolling yours! Remember, you can say a lot about yourself—and the God you serve—without ever saying a word.

Lord, help me to be careful not just with my words but also with all the things I say without saying a word. Let my face and my actions show the world my love—and Yours.

HOW GREAT!

It takes a lot of different muscles to make all those serious, smiling, and silly faces—43 different muscles in all. And while scientists don't agree on whether it takes more muscles to smile or to frown, there's one thing we can all agree on—a smile is much more beautiful than a frown!

WE'RE ALL IN THIS TOGETHER

Each one of us has a body, and that body has many parts. These parts all have different uses. In the same way, we are many, but in Christ we are all one body. Each one is a part of that body.

—ROMANS 12:4–5 ICB

Meerkats are amazing—especially in the way they work together. These squirrel-sized critters live together in groups called *mobs* or *gangs*. They not only work together to dig out the underground burrows they call home but also groom each other and hunt for food together. They even take turns babysitting and standing guard. But one of the most amazing ways they work together is when a predator attacks. If they can't make it back to their burrow, they'll all stand together as one, hissing and growling, so the predator knows it's facing something much bigger than just one little meerkat.

God made meerkats to work together. It's how He made us too. Each of us has different skills and a different job to do. And all are important—from the preacher to the window cleaner, from the singer to the sandwich maker. Whatever job God gives you to do, do it with all your heart and all your might. Be thankful for all the others who are doing their jobs too. Pray for each other, help each other, encourage each other. Because when we're attacked—by troubles, by sadness, or by the Devil himself—we're all stronger when we stand together!

If you've seen a meerkat standing up, you may have noticed their tummies don't have a lot of fur. You can even see their black skin showing through. That's no accident! After sleeping in a chilly burrow (deserts can get cold at night!), meerkats climb out and soak up the rays by standing up with their bellies to the Sun. The dark skin absorbs the heat and warms them right up.

Dear God, help me to find my place in Your church and kingdom. And remind me that everyone is special and has an important job to do for You.

MIRROR, MIRROR, ON THE . . . SALT?

"Those who hear the teaching of God and obey
it—they are the ones who are truly blessed."

—LUKE 11:28 ICB

"Mirror, mirror, on the wall"—that's how the fairytale goes. But if
you happen to be at the Salar de Uyuni (sa-LAR day uni) in South America,
you won't be asking about mirrors on the wall. That's because it's home to the

world's largest natural mirror. It's not hanging on the wall, and it's not made of glass. It's made of salt.

The Salar de Uyuni is the world's largest salt flat with more than 4,000 square miles of desert. Instead of sand, this desert has salt—at least 10 billion tons of it. It's so big and so white that it can be seen from space. NASA even uses it to help position its satellites. When it rains, the Salar de Uyuni is transformed into the most spectacular mirror, reflecting the sky back to itself. It's hard to tell where the "mirror" ends and the sky begins!

The Salar de Uyuni is an amazing natural mirror! But *you* can be an even more amazing mirror. How? By "reflecting" Jesus. Your life—everything you do and say—should be so filled with His love, truth, and goodness that people see Jesus reflected in you. For some people the "mirror" of your life might be the first glimpse of Jesus they see. But to mirror Jesus, you first have to know what He looks like. Read His Word. Look at how He lived. Do what He says— and you'll soon be reflecting Jesus for all the world to see.

Lord, let my life be so filled with Your truth and goodness that when people see me, they see You.

HOW GREAT!

Imagine sleeping on a bed made of . . . salt. Or sitting on a chair made of . . . salt. In a room where the walls are—you guessed it—made of salt! The Hotel De Sal Luna Salada and other hotels around the Salar de Uyuni are made almost entirely of salt, from the walls and ceilings to the furniture! But there's absolutely no licking allowed!

65

OH, THE POSSIBILITIES

Oh, Lord GOD, you made the skies and
the earth with your very great power.
There is nothing too hard for you to do.

— JEREMIAH 32:17 NCV

You've probably heard that bats are blind, but they aren't. In fact, some bats have excellent eyesight. But even with the best eyesight, finding all those thousands of tiny, flying insects they like to eat every night—*in the dark*—seems impossible. That's why God created bats with a special way of hearing that helps them "see" in the dark.

As the bats fly through the night skies, they make a sort of shouting sound that's so high-pitched humans can't hear it. That sound bounces (or *echoes*) off the buildings, trees, and insects around them, giving them a sort of map about whatever is up ahead. Bats can even tell the size and shape of a tiny mosquito, how far away it is, and which way it's going. This skill is called *echolocation* (EK-oh-loh-KAY-shun)—which simply means *locating* things by their *echo*. It gives bats the ability to track down dinner in the dark. And that's just one example of an impossible thing God has made possible.

Chances are you won't have to track down dinner in the dark—if you do, I really hope it's not bugs! But someday you will face an impossible task. That's when it's important to remember that impossible things become completely possible with God. So when God asks you to do something that seems impossible to you—like getting up in front of the whole church to say a prayer, talking to your new neighbor about Jesus, or forgiving that person who was hateful to you—don't focus on the impossible part. Focus on the

God who promises to give you everything you need to do what He asks you to do—even if it seems impossible.

> *God, some of the things You ask me to do are hard. Some of them even seem impossible. But Your Word says that nothing is impossible for You, so I trust You to work through me!*

HOW GREAT!

Bats are the only mammal that can actually fly. Some people think flying squirrels can fly, but they are only able to jump from trees and glide across to another tree or down to the ground. They can't fly on their own.

66

SO MUCH TO SEE!

Have you never heard? Have you never
understood? The LORD is the everlasting
God, the Creator of all the earth. He never
grows weak or weary. No one can measure
the depths of his understanding.

—ISAIAH 40:28 NLT

Exo comes from the Greek word that means "outside." Can you guess
what an exo*planet* might be? It's a planet outside our solar system that orbits

around a star just as the Earth orbits around the Sun. The first exoplanets were found in 1992. Now scientists have found more than 3,000 exoplanets, and they think there may be thousands more. Scientists searched for exoplanets using the Kepler Space Telescope, which was basically a massive telescope attached to a little spacecraft and sent off into space. The Kepler has now retired, but its discoveries changed the way scientists think about space and the planets in it.

The thing is, we'll never discover everything there is to know about space or the universe or all the galaxies and planets it contains. Building bigger telescopes just gives us the opportunity to discover more and more! Why? Because this unlimited universe was created by the unlimited God. Isaiah 40:28 says, "No one can measure the depths of his understanding"—or His creation. But even more amazing and wonderful than all the stars in the sky and all the exoplanets in the universe is this fact: we can also never measure the depths of His love for each of us.

Dear God, when I look up at the stars, I am so amazed by this universe that seems to never end. But I am even more amazed by Your love for me—and I'm so grateful to know that it will never end.

HOW GREAT!

Scientists have discovered a supermom galaxy. It's a place where stars are born. The thing that makes it so super is the fact that it gives birth to more new stars in a single day than our Milky Way does in an entire year. This supermom produces about 740 new stars a year, while the Milky Way births about only one new star a year. Now that's a super mom!

67

IN THE BLINK OF AN EYE

We will all be changed. It will only
take a second. We will be changed
as quickly as an eye blinks.

—1 CORINTHIANS 15:51–52 ICB

Blink. Blink. Blink. It's something we do about every 2 to 10 seconds. And it lasts about only one-tenth of a second. That's fast, but it's plenty of time for your eyelid to clear away any dust from your eyeball—kind of like a windshield wiper for your eyes. Blinking also coats your eyes with tears. Yes, even when you're not crying. The tears keep your eyes from drying out so that you can see more clearly.

Scientists have found that we tend to blink at certain times. When reading, we blink at the end of sentences. While watching a movie, we blink when the action changes. If we're listening to someone talk, we blink when they take a breath. Blinks give our brains a tiny rest.

Have you ever heard someone say, "In the blink of an eye"? It means that something will happen *really* quickly. And that's how fast the Bible says everything will change when Jesus comes back again. In the blink of an eye, He'll take you and all His children home to heaven. In the blink of an eye, He'll give you a new heart that will never know sadness and a new body that will never be sick. And in the blink of an eye, everything will be more wonderful than you could ever imagine. You'll be with God forever!

Lord Jesus, please wash away all my sins so that when You come again I can be with You in heaven—in the blink of an eye.

HOW GREAT!

Why doesn't your world go dark every time you blink? Because your brain is able to pretend you didn't close your eyes—and to remember what you saw right before you did. This lets you constantly see the world around you instead of seeing darkness every time you blink.

LET ME TELL YOU

Jesus said to the followers, "Go everywhere
in the world. Tell the Good News to everyone."

— MARK 16:15 ICB

**Animals might not have the same vocabulary as we do, but they
definitely have ways of getting their messages across.** Sometimes
they use their "voices" to bark, meow, hiss, or chirp. Other times they use

their bodies to say what they need to say. For example, when a scout bee spots a bunch of flowers filled with nectar, it flies back to the hive and does a little dance to tells all the other bees where to find them. The white-tailed deer warns other deer of possible danger by flicking up its tail—which is, you guessed it, white. Elephants say "I like you" by linking their trunks together, while gorillas tell you they're angry by sticking out their tongues.

God made sure animals can say what they need to say, and He made sure you can too. And the most important things God wants you to say are about Him: to tell people how much He loves them and how they can get to heaven one day. To do this, God gave you a mouth to speak and a mind to put the words together, and He'll also help you know what to say! He did it for Moses when he faced down the wicked pharaoh (Exodus 4:12), and He promises to do it for you too (Luke 12:12). Doesn't that just make you want to do a little dance?

Lord, I want to tell the whole world about You. Please give me the words that will help others see how great You really are!

Prairie dogs have quite a large vocabulary of yips and barks. In fact, they have a different "word" for every kind of predator they meet, including us. What's more, they use different "words" to describe how we look, what we're wearing, and how fast we move. So if you're ever stared at by a bunch of prairie dogs, then, yeah, they really are talking about you!

69

BE-*LEAF* IT OR NOT!

You are all one in Christ Jesus. And now that
you belong to Christ, you are . . . his heirs, and
God's promise to Abraham belongs to you.

— GALATIANS 3:28–29 NLT

It happens every fall. The leaves begin to change. Bright yellows and golds, glorious reds, even glowing oranges and purples take the place of all the green. Why does this happen? And how?

The tree is getting ready to rest for winter. All spring and summer, its leaves have been busy making food using a chemical called *chlorophyll* (KLOHR-uh-fil). That chemical gives the leaves their green color. There are yellow and orange colors in the leaves too, but the green hides them. In fall, as the days grow shorter and cooler, the leaves stop making food, the chlorophyll—and the green—disappears, and the yellow and orange colors show through. Other chemical changes happen in some trees. That's how we get all those amazing shades of red and purple.

If you just look around in fall, you'll know how much God loves colors. In fact, everywhere you look, you can see the different colors God created—in the flowers, in the skies, and even in us. There are so many colors of hair and eyes and skin. And they're all so beautiful! Some people only want friends that look and act just like them. That makes God sad and even angry. When you see someone who doesn't look quite like you, remember the most important thing about you is the same: you are both wonderfully and marvelously made by God (Psalm 139:14).

Dear God, when I see people who look different from me, help me remember that, just like me, they are Your prized creation. Thank You for making us so wonderfully unique!

HOW GREAT!

Leaves aren't the only things that change colors with the seasons. The Arctic hare, Siberian hamster, and Arctic fox are among the animals that change to a snowy white in winter—to better hide from predators!

Arctic fox

70

FROM BEGINNING TO END

"I am the Alpha and the Omega—the
beginning and the end," says the Lord God.
"I am the one who is, who always was, and
who is still to come—the Almighty One."

—REVELATION 1:8 NLT

Imagine a tree that was alive when Jesus was born here on Earth. When Jesus was healing the lepers, it was growing. When He told the storm to be quiet, it was growing. And it's *still* growing today!

You'll find not just one tree like that but several thousand Sierra redwood trees that are between 2,000 and 3,000 years old. There are even a few that are believed to be more than 4,000 years old! The Sierra redwood (also known as the giant sequoia) grows only in the Sierra Nevada mountain range in California. These trees usually grow to about 250 feet tall, but they can reach an amazing 300 feet tall or more—that's about the height of the Statue of Liberty! And many of these trees' trunks measure more than 94 feet around.

But as old and impressive as these trees are, they are nothing compared to God. He has always been alive—before the beginning of time. And He will be alive when Jesus comes again—and forever after that. You see, God is *eternal*. He has no beginning and no end. He has always been, and He will always be. That means He is always present in every moment of your life. And you can *always* count on Him.

God, it's hard for me to understand what eternity really means. But what I do understand is that You are always here with me. Thank You, God!

HOW GREAT!

One of the oldest trees ever found is called the Methuselah tree. It is named after the oldest man in the Bible (you can read about him in Genesis 5:21–27). The Methuselah is a great bristlecone pine tree and is believed to be more than 4,800 years old.

71

ARE YOU THIRSTY?

"Whoever drinks the water I give
will never be thirsty again."

— JOHN 4:14 ICB

You know deserts are dry. After all, they get only 10 inches of rain a year—or less! What you might not know is how many animals make their homes in the desert. God gave these animals amazing abilities to help them survive in the world's driest places.

Some—like scorpions, bats, and foxes—are *nocturnal*, which means they come out only at night, avoiding the heat of the day that dries them out. The

Peccary

peccary (a pig-like animal) has an especially tough mouth and tummy. It can chow down on water-rich cactuses, prickly spines and all! And the thorny devil lizard has spiky skin that soaks up water like a sponge. It can quench its thirst from the air, raindrops, or even mudpuddles.

Do you get thirsty? Not for water but for God? One day Jesus met a woman by a well in Samaria who was thirsty for God's love and forgiveness—though she didn't realize it. As she went to draw water up from the well, Jesus told her about a kind of living water that keeps you from being thirsty again. Now, Jesus wasn't talking about water that comes from a well or faucet. He was talking about the living water of His truth. You see, that Samaritan woman was thirsty for Someone to love and forgive her, despite all her mistakes. Jesus quenched her thirst with the truth that God loved her. And because she believed Him, He gave her the living water so she never had to be thirsty for God again (John 4:1–42).

Do you thirst for those things too? Then go to Jesus, talk to Him, trust and follow Him. He has living water for you too!

Lord, I know You are the God of all creation. I love You, I thirst for You, and I will always follow You. Please fill me up with the living water of Your love.

HOW GREAT!

The Australian water-holding frog stores water in its tissues, gills, and bladder—up to twice its body weight! It can then live up to five years without taking a drink. When it gets thirsty, it simply brings water from its bladder back up to its mouth to drink. *UGH!*

72

WHAT A BLAST!

The Lord gives strength to those
who are tired. He gives more power
to those who are weak.

—ISAIAH 40:29 ICB

The reason we don't all just float off into space is a thing called
gravity. It's this invisible force that pulls one object down to another object—
for example, the gravity of the Earth pulls your feet down to it. The bigger an
object is, the more gravity it has, so the Earth has a lot more gravity than the

Moon because it's a lot bigger than the Moon. That same gravity that keeps your feet on the ground, though, also keeps spacecraft on the ground. So how *do* spacecraft escape the pull of gravity? The answer is rocket power!

How do rockets work? Think of it this way: If you blow up a balloon and then let it go without tying a knot, what happens? It goes zooming off around the room, right? In the same way (but with lots more math and science added in), rockets are packed with fuel. As that fuel burns, it creates hot gases that blast out of the bottom so fast that they push the rocket (and the spacecraft it's attached to) up, up, up. That push is so powerful it's able to break away from the pull of gravity until it reaches space, where there is no gravity.

Rockets are powered by the fuel they carry inside them. And that's kind of the way you're powered—by the Holy Spirit inside you. You see, when you become a child of God—by believing, loving, and obeying Him—God sends His Holy Spirit to live inside you (1 Corinthians 3:16). The Spirit is your helper who teaches you more about God (John 14:26), helps you do what's right (Romans 8:14), and even helps you pray (Romans 8:26). He's the power of God inside you who helps you blast past the pull of sin, launching you right into the presence of God.

Lord, thank You for the Holy Spirit You've put inside me. Help me to count on His power to fuel me.

HOW GREAT!

Rockets were invented in China more than 800 years ago! The first ones were just simple tubes filled with gunpowder and stuck on a stick—a lot like our fireworks. The Chinese used them in battles against invading armies.

IT'S PINK!

"You must love each other as I have loved
you. All people will know that you are
my followers if you love each other."

— JOHN 13:34–35 ICB

Imagine standing at the edge of a lake, feeling the breeze on your face, and gazing out across the beautiful pink waters. Wait, what? *Pink* waters? Yep, that's right! If you're standing at the edge of Lake Retba in Senegal, you won't be gazing out over blue water. Instead, it's a bright bubblegum pink!

Lake Retba is separated from the Atlantic Ocean by just some narrow sand dunes, so it's *very* salty. Not much is able to live in it, except a bacteria called *Dunaliella salina*. In order to soak up the Sun, this little guy produces a red pigment—and it's that pigment that gives the lake its bright pink color.

Isn't it amazing how a bunch of tiny little bacteria can color an entire lake? What's even more amazing is how adding "tiny bits" of God and His love to your day can color your whole life! Thank God for His sunrise first thing in the morning, share a Bible verse at breakfast, or give a friend a helping hand with homework. As you share little bits of God, His Word, and His love all throughout your day, you'll be coloring the world with the greatness of your God!

While Lake Retba is a bubblegum pink, the Rocky Mountain Glacier Lakes stand out in colors of bright green and turquoise. They get their color from *rock flour*. This "flour" is created as rock is ground to a dust under the movement of glaciers. The rock flour is so light that it floats in the water, giving the lakes their beautiful, bright colors.

Lord, show me all the different, little ways I can color the world with Your love, Your Word, and Your greatness.

WHERE'S YOUR TREASURE?

"Store your treasure in heaven. The treasures in
heaven cannot be destroyed by moths or rust. And
thieves cannot break in and steal that treasure.
Your heart will be where your treasure is."

—MATTHEW 6:20–21 ICB

**You might not realize it, but there's a crime wave happening, possibly
right in your own backyard.** That's right! Squirrel bandits are stealing other
squirrels' nuts! To stop the widespread thievery, neighborhood squirrels have
taken to *lying* about their stashes. It's true! Squirrels will spy on their fellow nut

gatherers to see where they bury their stash. Then they'll sneak back and steal it. Squirrels can lose up to 25 percent of their nuts to thieves! To protect their food, squirrels will pretend to bury a nut but hide it in its mouth instead. They'll do this several times so that any watching squirrels won't know which hole the nut is actually in. Squirrels go to all this trouble because they count on their nuts to get them through the cold winter months when food is hard to find.

What are you counting on to see you through the tough times? A stash of nuts . . . I mean, treasures? Do you store up all the "stuff" of this world and save it just for yourself? If so, you might just find yourself acting a little squirrely, constantly scurrying around and worrying about your stuff. Instead of stashing away all that stuff you think you need, trust God to give you what you *really* need instead. Share your earthly treasures, and focus on storing up treasures in heaven. How? By trying to live the way Jesus did—loving God and doing good wherever He went. Be kind. Be generous. Share the cookie, share your time and friendship, share the good news about Him, and you'll have all the riches you'll ever need.

Lord, it's so easy to be selfish with my time and my things. Help me to focus on storing up treasures in heaven with You.

HOW GREAT!

Squirrels love to eat the acorns from oak trees, and they collect lots of them to nibble on during the winter. But because they bury them in several little stashes instead of one big stash, they sometimes forget exactly where they hid them, accidentally planting thousands of new trees every year. Just like Romans 8:28 says, God uses all things for good—even lost nuts!

75

LIKE NIGHT AND DAY

Teach us to number our days, that
we may gain a heart of wisdom.

—PSALM 90:12 NIV

Night and day. They just sort of happen, and we don't think much about them. Day is when the Sun is shining, and night is when it isn't, right? Right! But what *causes* day and night to happen? Well, it's all in how you spin it—the Earth, that is.

You don't feel it, but the Earth actually *spins* in space. Like a top. It's called *rotation*. It spins completely around once every 24 hours—or, to be exact, every 23 hours, 56 minutes, and 4.09 seconds. The part of the Earth facing the Sun has day, while the part facing away has night. As the Earth spins, day changes to night, and night changes to day. The in-between times become our morning and evening. Yes, it looks like the Sun is rising and setting, but the Sun isn't really moving at all—Earth is!

Here's the important thing, though: no matter how many hours of daylight or darkness there are, you have the same amount of time each day as everyone else. What are you going to do with those hours? Because the amount of sunlight shining into your world isn't nearly as important as the amount of God's light *you* shine into this world. Don't waste a moment. Day or night, love your neighbor, love God, and tell the world how awesome He is. Let His light shine!

Dear God, thank You for the wonder of day and night. Show me how to shine Your light into this world.

HOW GREAT!

Imagine not seeing the Sun for six months! That used to happen every year in the tiny town of Rjukan, Norway. Surrounded by mountains, not even a single ray of sunlight slipped in from September to March. Then, in 2013, the town positioned three giant mirrors on the mountaintop to capture the sunlight and reflect it down into the town's square. Now villagers can soak up the Sun!

76

DREAM A LITTLE DREAM

No one has ever seen this. No one has ever
heard about it. No one has ever imagined what
God has prepared for those who love him.

—1 CORINTHIANS 2:9 ICB

Scientists agree that everybody dreams. Even if people *say* they don't
dream, they really do. They just don't remember it! But *why* do we dream? No
one really knows!

Some scientists think dreams are a way of cleaning out your brain—tidying away things you should remember and tossing out all the extra bits of information you don't need. Others think dreams are your brain's way of working out problems you struggled with during the day. Still others (and this is the really boring theory) think dreams don't really *do* anything for you. They just kind of happen, like blinking.

Most dreams happen when you're in your deepest sleep. But some dreams happen when you're wide awake—they're the daydreams of what you would like to happen. Maybe it's winning the big game, being the star of the play, or becoming an astronaut. But do you ever dream of heaven? Of what it will be like? The Bible tells us there will be streets of gold and gates of jewels. No darkness or sickness or sadness ever. Just love and peace and light. All that will be wonderful. But the best part will be seeing Jesus face-to-face. And when you belong to God, that's a dream that really will come true!

Lord, thank You for the dream-come-true promise of heaven. There are so many things I can't wait to see, but most of all I can't wait to see You!

HOW GREAT!

Do animals dream? Yes! If you've ever watched a dog "chase" or bark at something in its sleep, you know they do. Lots of other kinds of animals dream too, including cats, rats, and even cuttlefish!

77

WHOOSHING AND SWOOSHING

Hold fast to the LORD your God.

—JOSHUA 23:8 NIV

Some words are extra good at painting a picture in your mind of what they mean. For example, if someone says the water whooshed and swooshed, you've probably got a pretty good idea of what it was doing. And it would probably look a lot like a whirlpool.

A *whirlpool* looks a lot like a funnel going down into the water. It forms when two streams of water—going in opposite directions—meet. Whirlpools

Saltstraumen maelstrom

can happen wherever water is flowing, from streams to oceans to your bathtub drain. Some whirlpools swirl around so fast that they can suck things down inside them. Those are called a *vortex*. Most whirlpools aren't strong enough to do any damage, but one kind is very powerful: the *maelstrom* (MEYL-struhm). The strongest maelstrom is the Saltstraumen near Norway. Every six hours it creates a whirlpool up to 33 feet wide and 16 feet deep that spins at 25 miles per hour. Small boats have to wait for the whirlpools to stop whirling before they can pass through!

Do you ever feel like you're stuck in a whirlpool? Everything is whirling and swirling around you—and you're getting tossed every which way. When that happens to you, don't panic. Grab hold of God and hold on tight. Remember the things He wants you to do: love Him and love others. Focus on those, and He'll help you sort out the rest. And don't worry—God won't ever let go!

Lord, when this world gets crazy and it seems like everything is spinning out of control, I'll hold tight to You. I know You're in control of every storm!

HOW GREAT!

In 1870, Jules Verne wrote a story called *Twenty Thousand Leagues Under the Sea*. In it, the *Nautilus* submarine was sucked into a deadly maelstrom off the coast of Norway. In real life, a maelstrom is no threat to large ships, though smaller fishing boats need to steer clear!

78

THE GREAT SPACE RACE

Your love, LORD, reaches to the heavens,
your faithfulness to the skies.

—PSALM 36:5 NIV

You've heard of car races and foot races, but did you know there was a space race? It started in the 1950s, and it was a race between the United States and Russia to see who could get into space and onto the Moon first. In 1957, the Russians took the lead by launching the first space satellite,

Apollo 11 launch

Sputnik 1. They quickly followed with the first man in space, Yury Gagarin, in 1961 and the first woman, Valentina Tereshkova, in 1963. But America was working hard as well. Alan B. Shepard Jr. became the first American in space in 1961. Then, just a few years later, Neil Armstrong, Michael Collins, and Buzz Aldrin launched off in the Apollo 11 spacecraft, headed for the Moon. On July 20, 1969, Neil Armstrong became the first man to walk on the Moon, and America took the lead!

Just imagine: Neil Armstrong traveled more than 238,000 miles just to step out on the Moon. That's one amazing trip! But it's not nearly as amazing as the trip Jesus made. He traveled all the way from heaven to step out on Earth, to live as a man, and to die on the cross. Why? Not to win a race but to win your heart and to save your soul. Because that's how much He loves you. How great is that?

Lord, every time I look up at the Moon, remind me that Your love for me reaches even farther than to the Moon and back again.

HOW GREAT!

When astronaut Neil Armstrong first saw the Earth from space, he said, "It suddenly struck me that that tiny pea, pretty and blue, was the Earth. I put up my thumb and shut one eye, and my thumb blotted out the planet Earth. I didn't feel like a giant. I felt very, very small." It's true. Compared to the hugeness of space, we are amazingly tiny. But we're amazingly important to God. Just check out Romans 8:38–39.

YOU CAN'T SEE ME

"No one can hide where I cannot
see him," says the Lord. "I fill all of
heaven and earth," says the Lord.

— JEREMIAH 23:24 ICB

It's a jungle out there! Or an ocean, or a forest, or . . . well, you get the picture. It's a wild world out there when you're an animal because there's always some other animal who thinks you look delicious. That's why God gave some

animals the ability to hide. For example, the baron caterpillar is green with lacy spikes that blend perfectly into the veins of a leaf. The pygmy seahorse has the exact same coloring and texture as the coral it lives in. In fact, we didn't even know it existed until 1969! And the top wings of the underwing moth look exactly like tree bark, making them practically impossible for predators to see.

God gave these animals the ability to hide. But you can never hide from God. Just ask Jonah. God told him to head east and preach to the Ninevites. But Jonah got on a boat headed west instead. God still saw him. One very large storm, a big heave-ho overboard, and a giant gulp later, Jonah found himself in the belly of a fish. And, yes, God saw him there too. (And Jonah learned his lesson. When the fish spit him out, he headed straight for Nineveh.) You just can't hide from God. And that's a good thing. Because God isn't just watching you; He's watching over you.

God, I'm so thankful for the way You watch over me. I don't ever want to try to hide from You.

HOW GREAT!

As tall as the giraffe is, you would think it would stick out—especially with all those polka-dot patches. But the giraffe is perfectly camouflaged for its African environment. Its height and its light and dark splotches blend in with the shadows of the tall trees, helping to hide it from predators like lions and hyenas.

BE THE SPARK!

Serve the Lord with all your heart.
Be joyful because you have hope.

—ROMANS 12:11–12 ICB

Rocks are pretty awesome—and useful. Builders build with them. Sculptors sculpt them. Jewelers . . . you get the idea. But did you know there's a rock that can start a fire? It's called *flint*. On the outside, it's white and lumpy, but when broken, it looks like shiny, dark glass. And it's hard. *Really* hard. But the thing flint is best known for is that if you strike two pieces together (or against steel), they create a spark. That spark can start a fire.

What are you best known for? Is it your love for God? You might have heard people talk about being "on fire" for God. That means you're so excited about God—loving Him, being loved by Him, and serving Him—that it just sort of "sparks" off you in everything you do and say. That spark can then spread to others.

The prophet Elijah was so "on fire" for God that he challenged the priests of the phony god Baal to a showdown. They would each pray, he said, and the god who sent fire first was the real God. Of course, our God—the only true God—won. When Elijah prayed, fire shot down from heaven. It was so hot that it even burned up the stones! (Read about it in 1 Kings 18:20–40.) Elijah was the spark that day because He stood up for God. Don't be afraid to speak up for God too. Be a spark today!

Dear Lord, please use me to show this world how awesome You are. Let me be the spark that sets someone else "on fire" for You.

HOW GREAT!

For centuries people have made use of flint's strength through a process called *flintknapping* in which flint stones are broken and shaped into a sharp edge or other useful shape. Knapped flint is used to make arrowheads, knives, drills, and other tools; in England, it's been used to build stone walls.

81

YAWWWN

I go to bed and sleep in peace.
Lord, only you keep me safe.

—PSALM 4:8 ICB

You've been yawning your whole life—even before you were born—but why? Well, it's a mystery. Scientists know *what* yawning is. It's an involuntary reflex, which means we can't control it. Yawning just happens.

But they don't know why we do it. Some think it cools off our brains so they don't get too hot. Others think it's a way to wake up our bodies because yawning makes our heart beat faster. Still others think it's to give ourselves an extra boost of oxygen. We yawn when we're sleepy, when we're bored, and sometimes for no real reason at all. It's one of those wonderful mysteries we'll have to ask God about when we get to heaven.

What isn't a mystery is the way God watches over each of us. Yes, you too! Whether you're sleepy, bored, wide awake, or somewhere in between. What does that mean for you? It means God always knows what's happening in your life, so He's right there to celebrate with you when great things happen. He's also there to help you when not-so-great things happen. And when it's time to sleep, He watches over you and keeps you safe all through the night. Because God is always there with you, you don't ever have to worry. And that's nothing to yawn about!

HOW GREAT!

Yawn. Yawn. *Yawn*. Did you just yawn? Chances are you did. That's because yawning is contagious. When you see someone yawning, or even see the word *yawn*, you'll soon be yawning yourself. Try this experiment. Write *yawn* on a piece of paper and stick it on your refrigerator. Then see how many of your family members yawn after they see it!

Lord, thank You for the way You watch over me—whether I'm wide awake, asleep, or yawning in between!

82

A TRIP AROUND THE SUN

"Before I formed you in the womb I knew you."

— JEREMIAH 1:5 NIV

Are you taking any big trips this year? Maybe a vacation or a trip to see your grandparents? You might not realize it, but you're actually taking a

monster of a trip right this very second! *How's that?* you ask. You're on a trip around the Sun. Just one lap around our Sun is about 584 million miles, and the trip will take you a whole year (or 365.242199 days to be exact). To make that trip in just one year, you'll be traveling more than 1,000 miles every 60 seconds. That's like traveling from New York to Florida in about the same time it takes to watch a couple of television commercials!

That's a really big trip! But you know what the greatest thing about it is? You're not taking it alone—not for one second of it. God is right there with you for every moment of the journey. In fact, He was there with you—knowing you, loving you, and making plans for you—even before you were born. He knows absolutely everything about you. And He knows what this journey of your life will hold today, tomorrow, and on every trip around the Sun you'll take. And because God already knows the future, He is able to give you exactly what you need to be ready for it. *That* is how great our God is!

Dear Lord, thank You for being with me for every moment of this trip around the Sun and through life. Teach me to see how great You are!

HOW GREAT!

God will give you everything you need for this trip around the Sun and through life. Just check out His promises in Jeremiah 29:11, Philippians 1:6, and Philippians 4:19. Try to memorize them this year!

FRIENDS FOREVER

"Love each other as I have loved you."

— JOHN 15:12 ICB

Elephants make fabulous friends. In an elephant herd, each seems to understand what the others are feeling. If one elephant is unhappy, the others will go to it and comfort it. Usually this means chirping softly and putting their trunks in its mouth. It's kind of a hug, elephant style. (Aren't you glad *we* don't hug that way?) If an elephant is hurt, the others will help it. And if one is threatened by a predator like a lion, the other elephants will form a

circle around it and defend it. Elephants are such good friends that if they are separated—even for years—they remember each other and rush to "hug" when they see each other again.

Comforting each other, helping each other, and protecting each other—that sounds like a pretty awesome definition of friendship, whether you're an elephant or not. Jesus said it this way: "Love each other as I have loved you." That's the secret to getting and keeping good friends. When a friend is hurting, offer comfort and hugs. If a friend needs help, go and help too! And if a friend is being attacked—by gossip, bullying, "frenemies," or just a really bad day—stand up for your friend. Stick together. That's what friends do. Pray for each other and share encouraging Scriptures from God's Word. By the way, that's what Jesus does for you. He's your friend forever—and what could be greater than that?

Lord, help me to love and comfort and stand up for my friends the way You love and comfort and stand up for me.

HOW GREAT!

Elephants are the world's largest land mammal. They can use their trunk like a snorkel to swim, and they can charge at almost 25 miles per hour. They're amazing animals. But there's one thing elephants can't do. Elephants can't jump!

ONE BIG MESS!

If we confess our sins, he will forgive
our sins. We can trust God. He does
what is right. He will make us clean
from all the wrongs we have done.

—1 JOHN 1:9 ICB

In the middle of the Pacific Ocean there's a nasty spot called the
Great Pacific Garbage Patch. It was formed as garbage got caught up
in the ocean currents that swirl in kind of a giant circle between Hawaii and
Japan.

Though it's sometimes called a garbage island, it's actually more like a garbage soup made up of lost fishing nets, bags, bottles, and tiny bits of plastic.
It's at least the size of Texas—maybe bigger! The Garbage Patch is dangerous

because birds, turtles, and other sea animals get tangled in it or mistake it for food. As many as 1 million sea birds and 10,000 other sea animals die in it or because of it every year.

Probably no one gave a thought to that water bottle they tossed off the boat or to the plastic bag that blew away with the wind. They're just little things, after all. But the Great Pacific Garbage Patch proves that little things can add up to a big mess! And so can sin. You might not think that one little fib about forgotten homework would matter. Or that it would make a difference to watch that TV show all your friends are watching, even though your parents said not to. But little sins—little ways you take part in the evil of this world—add up. And before you know it, you've got one big mess. Avoid the mess by avoiding the sin. It's much easier than trying to clean up a garbage patch!

Lord, help me to stay away from the little sins so that I can stay out of big messes!

HOW GREAT!

You can help keep the Garbage Patch—and other pollution spots—from getting bigger by not using so many throwaway plastics, like plastic forks, cups, and plates. Use cloth shopping bags instead of plastic. Grab a reusable water bottle instead of the throwaway ones. Recycle plastics as much as you can. Because all of us doing little good things adds up to big improvements!

MONKEY SEE, MONKEY DO

"Accept my teachings and learn from me,
because I am gentle and humble in spirit,
and you will find rest for your lives."

— MATTHEW 11:29 NCV

Have you ever heard the saying, "Monkey see, monkey do"? It means we tend to do what we see others do. It's actually a pretty good way to teach— and not just for monkeys. The orangutan mom keeps her babies with her until

they're about eight years old, letting them watch and then practice the skills they'll need to survive—like knowing what foods are safe to eat, how to find them, and how to build a nest. Polar bear moms teach their cubs how to stay warm in their frozen world. And the cheetah mom teaches her cubs to hunt by letting them watch her in action. Later she'll let them join her on a hunt, gradually teaching them all they need to know to survive.

Watching and learning works for us humans too. That's why Jesus came—so that we could watch and learn the way to live, the way to love, and the way to heaven. Read your Bible, "watch" the way Jesus did things, and practice them for yourself. Don't worry if you make a mistake. He won't get angry. He's always ready to give you another chance to get it right. Because Jesus is the world's greatest teacher!

Jesus, help me to learn from Your example, to live the way You did, and to love the way You do. I want to be more and more like You.

HOW GREAT!

It's no real surprise that animals like orangutans and cheetahs are good parents, but what about the python? Surprisingly, these monster snakes stay with their eggs (all 40 to 50 of them), keeping them warm until  they hatch about 53–55 days after being laid. Even after, the mothers stay with their young and protect them for about two weeks. After that, those kids are on their own!

RUMBLE, BA-RUMBLE, BADABOOM!

When he thunders, the waters in the heavens roar; he makes clouds rise from the ends of the earth. He sends lightning with the rain and brings out the wind from his storehouses.

— JEREMIAH 10:13 NIV

Boom! The windows rattle and your heart jumps. *Rumble, ba-rumble, badaboom!* What is that crashing, cracking sound? It's not an explosion—it's thunder.

Thunder is caused by lightning. You see, when lightning zips through the sky, it heats up the air around it to more than *48,000 degrees Fahrenheit!* (That's hotter than the surface of the Sun!) Anytime it's heated, air gradually expands—or takes up more space. But when lightning strikes, the air heats up and expands so quickly that it explodes out in waves traveling close to the speed of sound. The hot air then cools quickly, causing the expanded air to contract. The fast-moving air is what creates the boom!

If you've ever watched a thunderstorm roll in, you know how powerful they are. Now just think of the power of the God who created all that! He's the One who controls the storms (Job 28:26). He "makes clouds rise" and "sends lightning with the rain." He is the God of thunder! (Sorry, not sorry, Thor!) So no matter how big the storm is, how often the lightning flashes, or how loud the thunder booms, you don't have to be afraid. The One who is the Lord and Creator of it all is watching over you.

Can lightning strike the same place twice? Yes! There are more than 1.5 billion lightning strikes on the Earth every year. Tall places like buildings, utility poles, and trees can be struck multiple times. One famous example is the Empire State Building in New York City. It gets struck an average of 23 times a year!

God, whenever I see the power of lightning, I'll remember that You are even more powerful. And when I hear the boom of thunder, I'll remember to listen to You.

177

A WALK IN THE PARK

"I am the light of the world. Whoever
follows me will never walk in darkness,
but will have the light of life."

— JOHN 8:12 NIV

Have you ever heard the phrase "a walk in the park"? It means that something will be easy to do. If you've played your favorite video game over and over, playing the first level again would be easy—a walk in the park. But

doing something for the first time is often hard, like landing on the Moon. On May 25, 1961, President John F. Kennedy announced his ten-year goal to have the United States land a man on the Moon and return him safely. That finally happened on July 20, 1969, but not without trouble. As astronauts Neil Armstrong and Buzz Aldrin began to land, the onboard computer overloaded, setting off an alarm, and their communication connection to Mission Control kept fading in and out. They considered calling off the mission, but that option was just as dangerous at that point. To top it all off, they only had enough fuel for one landing, so they had to get it right the first time. It was no walk in the park, but the Apollo 11 mission was a huge success for all of mankind.

Even better than the mission to land on the Moon is the mission to follow Jesus. The Bible shows how Jesus lived and how He loved God and others. And when we do what He did, we're fulfilling our mission. God knows you'll run into trouble and need help along the way, so don't worry—unlike Mission Control, your communication connection with Him will never fade. Your mission may not be a walk in the park, but it's the greatest mission of all time.

Lord, each day help me to follow in Jesus' footsteps—to help like Him, talk like Him, and love like Him.

HOW GREAT!

NASA astronauts are headed back to the Moon in the near future—and this time they're going to stay for a while! NASA plans to build an outpost called the Gateway that will orbit the Moon. Astronauts will be able to live there while exploring and training on the Moon. The Gateway may even be used to launch future missions all the way to Mars.

WHAT'S OLD IS
NEW AGAIN

"For God loved the world so much that
he gave his only Son. God gave his Son
so that whoever believes in him may
not be lost, but have eternal life."

— JOHN 3:16 ICB

Nothing on this Earth lives forever, right? Well, not exactly. There's this one jellyfish that kind of does. It's called the immortal jellyfish, or *Turritopsis Dohrnii*. (Don't worry, I can't say it either!) It's tinier than the tip of your pinkie finger and lives in the Mediterranean Sea. The amazing thing about this little jellyfish is that if it gets hurt or is threatened or in danger of starving, it shrinks itself into a tiny, gooey blob. And that's when things get *really* interesting. The jellyfish's adult cells transform back into baby cells, and within just a few days, it's like a newborn baby again! How great is that?

The immortal jellyfish's name is a bit misleading because it isn't really immortal. It won't live for all eternity, but if you've put your trust in Jesus, you will! Because Jesus came not only to take away your sins but also to give you eternal life. And not just life like your life on Earth but life in heaven with Him! All He asks is that you believe Jesus is the Son of God, that you love Him, and that you obey His commands. And He even promises to help you do all those things! Just imagine—heaven, forever, with Jesus. Revelation 21 tells a little bit about what heaven will be like. A place with no tears, pain, or death. A place where God will live with His people! It really doesn't get any greater than that!

God, it's hard to even imagine how long forever is, but I'm so thankful that I get to spend it in heaven with You!

HOW GREAT!

Jellyfish aren't really made of jelly. And they aren't fish. They're actually a sort of cousin to coral. Their bodies are made almost completely of water—about 90 percent water. They don't have bones or brains or hearts. Basically, they're just a floating mouth with tentacles.

89

LOOK TO THE SKIES!

The Lord showed [the Israelites] the way. During the day he went ahead of them in a pillar of cloud. And during the night the Lord was in a pillar of fire to give them light.

—EXODUS 13:21 ICB

Clouds come in all shapes, colors, and sizes. There are puffy, white clouds and dark, gloomy, booming thunderclouds. All those different shapes, colors, and sizes can tell us a lot about the weather that's coming our way.

Wispy, white clouds are called *cirrus* (SIR-uhs), and they usually mean the weather is going to change soon. *Stratus* (STRAT-uhs) clouds are thick and gray, often covering the whole sky. They mean rain or snow is on the way. Those puffy, white clouds are *cumulus* (KYOO-myuh-luhs), and they mean good weather is here. So if you want a clue about what the weather will be, look to the skies.

Cirrus clouds

Cumulus clouds

Stratus clouds

In the Old Testament, the Israelites also looked to the skies—not for weather but for directions. You see, when they escaped from slavery in Egypt, God led them with a pillar of cloud. At night it became a pillar of fire, so they would know that He was with them even in darkness.

There will be times when you don't know which way to go. That's when you need to look to God because He will lead you too. Probably not in a pillar of cloud, but wouldn't that be cool? God may not show you how everything will turn out—He certainly didn't for the Israelites—but He will show you the next step to take, and then the next, and the next—all the way home to heaven. How great is that?

God, when I look up and see the clouds, help me remember that I should always look to You to lead me.

HOW GREAT!

Clouds are made of millions and *bajillions* (a not-so-scientific word that means "a whole lot") of tiny water droplets floating in the air. How did those water droplets get there? They began as water vapor, which is invisible and always floating around in the air. As temperatures cool, that vapor *condenses* (or collects) on bits of dust to make water droplets, which then gather together to form clouds.

90

EVERYTHING YOU NEED

I pray that God, the source of hope,
will fill you completely with joy and
peace because you trust in him.

—ROMANS 15:13 NLT

Bromeliads (broh-MEE-lee-ads) are unusual and *fascinating* plants. The most interesting ones are *tank bromeliads*, and they live in the rainforest. Their leaves grow in a tight circle, forming a kind of cup, or tank, that collects and holds rainwater. Some bromeliads are so large that their tanks can hold up to five gallons of water! Those water tanks become a sort of world of their own with all sorts of creatures living inside—from fungi and algae to insects, spiders, and scorpions. You might also find frogs, salamanders, and snakes living in the pool of a bromeliad. In exchange for their home, the animals feed the bromeliads with their waste. Some of the creatures live their whole lives inside the bromeliad. It has everything they need.

Kind of like how God has everything you need. When you trust God, He becomes your "source of hope"—which means you can know that all those good things He's promised you, like heaven, really are coming your way. And trusting God isn't like trusting the people of this world. Even the best people aren't perfect and can let you down sometimes. But God never does. He keeps every single one of His promises. And one of those promises is to give you everything you need (Philippians 4:19). How great is that?

The poison-arrow frog uses bromeliads like a nursery. After the eggs hatch into tadpoles, the mother frog carries them to a bromeliad. She puts each tadpole in its own little pool of water between the bromeliad's leaves. There, they munch on algae and insect larvae while swimming in the safety of the bromeliad's waters.

Lord, You are the source of every good thing. I know I can trust You to give me everything I need.

185

91

MELTING ROCKS AND HEARTS

The glory of the LORD looked like a
consuming fire on top of the mountain.

—EXODUS 24:17 NIV

Lava. It's the perfect ingredient for a Hollywood disaster movie. But what is it? Lava is magma. *Okay,* you say, *what's magma?* Magma is superhot, melted rock—just like lava. You see, it's all about location. Melted rock that's underground is called magma. Once the magma moves above ground, it's called lava. Lava usually comes from an erupting volcano, but it can also seep up through cracks in the Earth's surface.

Lava can be thick and slow, moving only inches a day, or it can be so thin that it races downhill at 35 miles per hour! It all depends on the amount of gas dissolved in the lava and the slope of the land it's moving down. Lava can be as hot as 2,200 degrees Fahrenheit. As that hot lava meets cooler air, it begins to harden into a kind of rock called *igneous* (IG-nee-us). The Hawaiian Islands were formed by underwater lava piling higher and higher until the islands rose up out of the sea.

Just imagine: God is so powerful He can melt rocks and then use those melted rocks to make islands. But God's even better at melting our hardened hearts . . . with His love. A love so big that there's enough for every single person on Earth (2 Peter 3:9). A love so strong that nothing can tear it away from you (Romans 8:38–39). And a love so powerful that God sent His own Son, Jesus, to die to save you (1 John 4:9). Let God's love melt your heart—and follow Him today.

Lord, the difficult things in my life can make my heart feel hard. I pray that You would melt my heart with Your strong and sure love; make it completely Yours.

HOW GREAT!

There's actually a supervolcano underneath Yellowstone National Park that has enough magma in it to fill up the Grand Canyon more than 11 times! But don't worry; scientists think its chances of erupting are about 1 in 700,000.

92

WHAT TIME IS IT?

"This is the LORD's sign to you that the LORD
will do what he has promised: I will make the
shadow cast by the sun go back the ten steps
it has gone down on the stairway of Ahaz."

—ISAIAH 38:7-8 NIV

When you want to know what time it is, do you look at a clock or a watch or maybe a phone? Well, ancient Egyptians didn't have any of those things, so they invented the sundial—about 3,500 years before Jesus was born! It was the first time-telling instrument, and people still use sundials today. They work by using the shadows cast by the Sun.

The flat part of a sundial (called the *dial plate*) has marks on it for each hour of sunlight. A piece called a *gnomon* (NO-man) sticks up from the dial plate. The Sun's rays hit the gnomon and cast a shadow on one of the marks on the dial plate. That mark tells you what time it is. As the Sun moves, the shadow moves so you always know the time.

Because the Earth always moves around the Sun in the same direction, a shadow—on or off a sundial—always moves in the same direction. Well, not *always*. There was one time when it didn't! Second Kings 20 tells the story of when good King Hezekiah was very sick. He wept and prayed and begged God to heal him. At last God said Hezekiah would live for 15 more years! But Hezekiah asked for a sign to prove this would really happen. A great stairway stood nearby, and the Lord made the shadow climb *backward* 10 steps. Then Hezekiah knew he had been given a promise from God. Only our great God could make a shadow go backward!

The Vrihat Samrat Yantra (which means "the great king of instruments") in Jaipur, India, is the world's largest sundial. Built in 1738, it is almost 90 feet tall and is accurate to within two seconds. The shadow moves about one millimeter (or about the thickness of a dime) every second.

Lord, You are amazing. Not only did You make the Sun and the shadows, but You can make them go backward. Only You can do something that great!

189

93

GERMY GERMS!

"I am the Lord who heals you."

— EXODUS 15:26 ICB

Spit. Tears. Skin. Mucus (also known as snot). Even special blood cells. They all work together as part of your *immune system* to fight off germs.

Germs are tiny little organisms—yes, they're alive! They're so small you need a microscope to see them. Germs constantly attack your body, trying to sneak in through your eyes and nose, cuts and scrapes, and in lots of other ways. Your immune system works hard to fight them off. And if a germ does make you sick, your immune system keeps battling to heal your body.

When Jesus was living here on Earth, He did a lot of healing. People with sicknesses of every kind came to Him. One day, four friends tried to carry a paralyzed man to Jesus. But there were so many people gathered in the house where Jesus was that they couldn't even get inside. Instead of giving up, they climbed up on the roof, cut a hole, and lowered their friend down—right in front of Jesus! (Read about it in Luke 5:17–26.) Jesus did heal that man, but first, He did something even more important. He said, "Your sins are forgiven." Why? Because the sickness of sin—all the wrong things we've done—is much more serious than any sickness of the body. Our bodies can only be sick here on Earth, but our souls can be sick with sin for all eternity. Jesus came to heal us of our sins. So if you realize you've sinned, be like that man and his friends— don't let anything stop you from getting to Jesus. Stop right where you are and ask Him to forgive you. He will. Every single time (1 John 1:9).

Lord, thank You for all the ways You keep my body healthy and strong. But most of all, thank You for healing me of the sickness of sin.

HOW GREAT!

Allergies happen when your immune system gets confused. Sometimes it thinks "harmless" things, like cat hair, peanut butter, eggs, or even blooming flowers are germs, and it starts to fight them. That's when your eyes itch or your nose starts running. Fortunately, doctors have figured out ways to tell the immune system to chill out!

THAT'S POWERFUL STUFF!

"If your faith is as big as a mustard seed,
you can say to this mountain, 'Move from
here to there.' And the mountain will move.
All things will be possible for you."

—MATTHEW 17:20 ICB

When you get plopped on the nose by a raindrop, you probably don't think, *Wow! This is powerful stuff!* But when a whole bunch of water gathers together and comes crashing down, like it does in a waterfall, it is an incredibly powerful thing.

Waterfalls are created when water . . . well . . . falls over a rock wall. That wall may be carved out by a stream or river that flows over the rock and wears it away over many years. Or it may be formed by a glacier (a giant sheet of ice) slowly cutting the rock away. Or it might be created in an instant by an earthquake, a volcanic eruption, or a landslide that causes big chunks of rock to suddenly shift and fall away. Waterfalls can be a tiny trickle or a massive, roaring wonder—like the world-famous Niagara Falls, which has 757,500 gallons of water flowing over its top every second! The power of large waterfalls can be tapped to produce electricity, but even the smallest waterfalls have the power to shape the world around them.

Kind of like faith. When you believe God is who He says He is and will do all the things He says He'll do, that's called faith. But your faith doesn't have to be huge—or perfect—to shape the world around you. In fact, Jesus said that even faith the size of a mustard seed (which is about one to two millimeters or the thickness of a penny) is powerful enough to move a mountain. That's because the power isn't in the size of *your* faith. The power is in the One

192

you put your faith in. And God is able to take a mustard-seed-sized faith—or a raindrop-sized one—and turn it into a rushing, roaring waterfall that's powerful enough to shape you and the world around you. Now *that* is powerful stuff!

Lord, I believe You can move the mountains in my life. Please help me to have faith in Your amazing power.

Angel Falls, Venezuela

HOW GREAT!

The tallest waterfall in the world is Angel Falls in Venezuela. It's 3,212 feet tall—that's taller than three Eiffel Towers stacked on top of each other! But the biggest is Khone Falls in the country of Laos. It's more than 35,000 feet wide, and 2,500,000 gallons of water flow over every second!

95

NOSEY, NOSEY!

Do not let selfishness or pride be your
guide. Be humble and give more honor
to others than to yourselves.

—PHILIPPIANS 2:3 ICB

Big or small, hooked or pointed, noses come in all shapes and sizes—especially animal noses. And they aren't just for breathing and smelling. They're for digging! Yep, *digging*. If you're a mole, that is. You see, the mole is practically blind. But special "fingers" on its nose help it "see" in the underground burrows where it lives. Those "fingers" also help the mole dig its burrows by loosening the dirt right in front of it, which the mole then moves out of the way with its claws. Aren't you glad you don't have to dig out a place to live with your nose?

Even though your nose isn't much good for digging, it can do a few different jobs too—from smelling to breathing to holding up your sunglasses! But there's one thing you should never use your nose for, and that's looking down on others. Romans 12:16 warns us not to be too proud to show kindness to others. And we shouldn't go around thinking we're smarter than everyone else either. Instead, we should be humble and treat others as if they are better than we are (Philippians 2:3). That's what Jesus did. He was the Son of God, but He touched lepers, talked to tax collectors, and even washed His disciples' feet! Jesus was perfect, yet He didn't look down His nose at anyone—and neither should you!

Lord, You gave me this gift of life. Please teach me how to make my life a gift back to You and to everyone around me.

HOW GREAT!

The star-nosed mole has a nose that looks like, well, a star! The 22 "fingers" arranged around its nose make it look like a spiky star. But those fingers are so sensitive that they can sense when an earthquake or volcanic eruption is about to happen. This guy's nose really knows!

SOAK UP THE SON

The LORD is near to all who call on him,
to all who call on him in truth.

—PSALM 145:18 NIV

You've heard of imaginary friends and imaginary stories, right? But did you know there's an imaginary line all the way around the Earth? It's called the equator, and it circles around the center of the earth—like a belt—halfway between the North and South Poles. That belt is about 24,900 miles around!

Because the Earth is round and a little tilted in space, the Sun's rays fall straight down on the equator. That makes the weather stay warm there all year

long. The North and South Poles don't get as much of the Sun's rays, so they stay much colder.

With all that sunlight, the weather around the equator is hot—though it's not as hot as you might think. It's "only" about 68 to 86 degrees Fahrenheit in most places. However, the equator gets about 80 inches of rain a year, which keeps the air filled with moisture, or humidity, making it feel much hotter.

The equator is very different from the rest of the Earth because it gets more of the Sun. In the same way, when you get more of the Son—Jesus the Son, that is—you'll be very different from the rest of the world too. And that's a great thing! But how do you get more Jesus? Easy—just spend time with Him. Sit with Him. Talk to Him. The Bible promises that if you draw near to Him, He'll draw near to you too (James 4:8). So take a walk, have a talk with Jesus, and soak up the Son.

Jesus, I want to soak up as much of You as I can. Teach my heart to love You more and more each day.

HOW GREAT!

It's a fact that the higher up you go, the cooler the temperature gets—even at the equator. But did you know that if you climb up to the top of the mountains near the equator, you can actually find snow? And on Mount Kilimanjaro in Tanzania, about 200 miles south from the equator, you'll even find ice!

Mount Kilimanjaro

97

THE POWER OF BLOOD

If we are living in the light, as God is in
the light, then we have fellowship with
each other, and the blood of Jesus,
his Son, cleanses us from all sin.

—1 JOHN 1:7 NLT

Blood. Some people faint at the sight of it, but you couldn't live without it! Blood is made up of red and white blood cells floating in a liquid called *plasma*.

The red blood cells are a kind of delivery system. They carry oxygen and other nutrients to all the cells in your body, and then they carry away all the waste, like carbon dioxide. Blood is pumped through your body by the heart. Your heart is one strong muscle, and it's fast too—it can pump blood to every cell in your body in less than a minute! Blood travels through tubes called *blood vessels*. The vessels that carry blood away from your heart are called *arteries*, while the ones that carry it back to your heart are called *veins*. The white blood cells are the warrior cells. They work together with your immune system (check out page 190) to fight off germs and diseases.

Your blood is pretty powerful and important stuff! But the blood of Jesus is even more powerful. Because He is the Son of God, lived a perfect life, and never sinned—not even one single time—His blood can carry your sins away and give you the forgiveness you need to live forever with God. All you have to do is believe and obey Him. When Jesus gave His life for you on the cross, it was both terrible and beautiful—terrible for the way Jesus was hurt, but so beautiful for the gift of love and forgiveness and heaven He gave to you and me.

Lord, it's hard to think about Jesus' death on the cross, and I'm so sorry for all He suffered. But I am so grateful for His blood that washes my sins away.

HOW GREAT!

Platelets are another very important part of your blood. (You say it the way it looks: PLATE-let.) When you get a cut or scrape, these little guys spring into action, sticking together to stop the flow of blood—called *clotting*. They not only keep blood inside your body but also keep germs out!

98

NO CLOWNING AROUND

The Lord is faithful. He will give you strength
and protect you from the Evil One.

—2 THESSALONIANS 3:3 ICB

The clownfish has become quite the movie star in recent years. But this little guy deserves its fame. It makes its home among the tentacles of a sea anemone (uh-NEM-uh-nee). The anemone looks like an underwater flower, but it's really an animal—*with poisonous, stinging tentacles!* That's right, the clownfish lives in a world of poison. How does it survive? God gave the

clownfish a special layer of mucus on its skin, which protects it from the anemone's stings. And check this out: the clownfish actually helps the anemone by keeping it clean and chasing off any predators that might want to have an anemone for lunch.

You are actually a lot like a clownfish. No, I don't mean you have orange and black stripes. But you do live in a poisonous world that is filled with sin—and with temptations for you to sin. But when you become a child of God, He gives you protection from the poison. He not only helps you stand strong against the evils of this world but also protects you from the evil one (2 Thessalonians 3:3), fights for you (Deuteronomy 20:4), and promises that the Devil can never snatch you away from Him (John 10:28). Pretty cool, huh?

Oh . . . and there's one more way you're like a clownfish. You can help clean up your poisonous world too—by sharing the message of all that God can do.

Lord, thank You for protecting me from the poisons of this world. And please help me to do what I can to clean it up.

HOW GREAT!

When a percula clownfish is looking for an anemone to call home, it doesn't just barge right in. It does a little dance to introduce itself. And by carefully touching first its fins and then other parts of its body to the stinging tentacles, the clownfish is able to get used to the anemone's stings.

99

RIVER OF LIFE

"Blessed is the man who trusts in the
LORD, and whose hope is the LORD. For he
shall be like a tree planted by the waters,
which spreads out its roots by the river."

— JEREMIAH 17:7–8 NKJV

We swim in them, boat on them, drink from them, and even get
power from them. What are they? Rivers! There are 165 major rivers across

the world—and thousands upon thousands of smaller ones. There are roughly 250,000 rivers in the United States alone. If you added together their lengths, it would total more than 3,500,000 miles. That's enough to stretch to the Moon and back again seven times!

Nile River

The Nile River in Africa is the longest river in the world at more than 4,160 miles long. The Amazon River in South America is the second longest at nearly 4,000 miles long. Compare that to America's Mississippi River, which is "only" about 2,350 miles long.

A river is a stream of water—usually pretty big—that flows across the land and gives life to it. Many of the earliest cities and towns were established near a river because they were so important to life. There was even a river in the garden of Eden (Genesis 2:10)! Rivers give people water for drinking and washing as well as fish and other foods to eat. They were the earliest highways, giving people an easy way to travel. Today, many cities and towns are still located near rivers. Even though rivers make up only a tiny fraction of the total water on Earth, God uses them in mighty ways to provide life for His creation.

Just as rivers give life to the land, God gives life to His people. And just as water flows down a river, God's peace will flow through you when you trust and follow Him. His peace is more than just a warm, comfortable feeling. It's the strength to keep going when you're tired. It's the courage to do what's right—even when no one else will. Peace is knowing that God is always there to help you, guide you, and give you whatever you need to keep following Him.

Lord, please let Your peace—Your strength and courage and love— flow through my whole life, just like water flows through a river.

SLEEP ON IT

"Keep watch, because you do not know
on what day your Lord will come."

—MATTHEW 24:42 NIV

If you've ever burrowed under the covers for a nap on a cold day, you might have been accused of hibernating. But that wouldn't be exactly right. Hibernation is much different from taking a nap. It's a way to stay alive. You see, in winter, when temperatures are cold and food is hard to

find, animals either move to a warmer place with more food (called *migrating*) or they stay put. Some animals that stay put hibernate so they need less food and warmth to survive. There are animals—like ground squirrels—that find a safe spot and don't move until warm weather comes again. They barely even breathe! Others—like bears and skunks—wake up now and then, even going out for a walk or a snack.

Sometimes this world gets pretty cold. Not in terms of temperature but in how tough life can be. And there are days when it would be nice to just hide out in bed. But that's not something we can do. Our job—as followers of Jesus—is to get out there in the world, to tell the world about Jesus, and to show them how much He loves each and every person (Matthew 28:19–20). There are a lot of people who don't know about Jesus and how awesome He is, so there's no time for hibernating on the job. Do something good, say something kind, and lend a helping hand every chance you get (Ephesians 5:16)!

Dear God, I know that one day Jesus will come back. Help me to be ready—and help me to live a life that will make others want to meet Him too.

Animals hibernate in surprising ways. Some species of snakes gather in groups of hundreds or even thousands to stay warm. Water turtles bury themselves in mud at the bottom of a pond, while land turtles burrow into the ground to hibernate. Snails coat themselves in mucus before burying themselves. They even coat their shells with mucus, which keeps others from entering during the cold months.

INDEX

LOUIE GIGLIO is the pastor of Passion City Church and the original visionary of the Passion movement, which exists to call a generation to leverage their lives for the fame of Jesus. Since 1997, Passion has gathered collegiate-aged young people in events across the US and around the world, and it continues to see 18–25-year-olds fill venues across the nation. Most recently, Passion hosted 40,000 college students and their leaders in four venues linked together across three cities at Passion 2019. In addition to the Passion Conferences, Louie and his wife, Shelley, lead the teams at Passion City Church, sixstepsrecords, Passion Publishing, and the Passion Global Institute. Louie is the national bestselling author of *Not Forsaken*, *Goliath Must Fall*, *Indescribable: 100 Devotions About God & Science*, and *The Comeback*. Louie and Shelley make their home in Atlanta, Georgia.

NICOLA ANDERSON has been an illustrator and graphic designer since she could hold a crayon in her hand but has been working professionally since 2001. After many years working in the design industry, she now crafts imaginary worlds from her home studio, AndoTwin Studio, in Manchester, UK. During this time, she has worked with an eclectic range of clients and has loved every minute!

Published in Nashville, Tennessee, by Tommy Nelson. Tommy Nelson is an imprint of Thomas Nelson. Thomas Nelson is a registered trademark of HarperCollins Christian Publishing, Inc.

Written by Louie Giglio with Tama Fortner. Illustrated by Nicola Anderson.

All images © Shutterstock unless otherwise noted. The Witch Head Nebula, page 23, NASA/STScI Digitized Sky Survey, processed into a full-color image by Noel Carboni. Pages 71, 93, 105, 127, and 205 images © iStock.

Tommy Nelson titles may be purchased in bulk for educational, business, fund-raising, or sales promotional use. For information, please email SpecialMarkets@ThomasNelson.com.

Scripture quotations marked ICB are taken from the International Children's Bible®. Copyright © 1986, 1988, 1999, 2015 by Thomas Nelson. Used by permission. All rights reserved. Scripture quotations marked NCV are taken from the New Century Version®. © 2005 by Thomas Nelson. Used by permission. All rights reserved. Scripture quotations marked NIV are taken from the Holy Bible, New International Version®, NIV®. Copyright © 1973, 1978, 1984, 2011 by Biblica, Inc.® Used by permission of Zondervan. All rights reserved worldwide. www.zondervan.com. The "NIV" and "New International Version" are trademarks registered in the United States Patent and Trademark Office by Biblica, Inc.® Scripture quotations marked NKJV are taken from the New King James Version®. © 1982 by Thomas Nelson. Used by permission. All rights reserved. Scripture quotations marked NLT are taken from the Holy Bible, New Living Translation. © 1996, 2004, 2007, 2013 by Tyndale House Foundation. Used by permission of Tyndale House Publishers, Inc., Carol Stream, Illinois 60188. All rights reserved.

Library of Congress Cataloging-in-Publication Data is on file.

ISBN-13: 978-1-4002-1552-2

Printed in Bosnia and Herzegovina

23 24 25 GPS 15 14

ISBN: 978-1-4002-3588-9

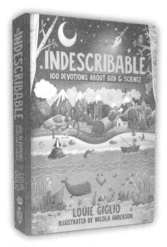

ISBN: 978-0-7180-8610-7

ISBN: 978-1-4002-3046-4

If you loved Pastor Louie's *How Great Is Our God*, then check out *Indescribable, The Wonder of Creation,* and *Indescribable Activity Book for Kids.*

Visit IndescribableKids.com to learn more!